shit adults never taught us

NATASHA SATTLER

Shit Adults Never Taught Us
Copyright © 2021 by Natasha Sattler

This work contains factual information as well as anecdotal information. All names have been changed and identities concealed to protect individuals where applicable.

All corporations, companies and entities mentioned are purely on a subjective basis and in context to the information provided. No sponsorship or brand collaboration was done in partnership with this book, neither paid nor unpaid. No brand was approached for recognition nor has the writer received any benefits for the usage of a certain brand or company mentioned.

Grateful acknowledgement is made to all those who have allowed for permission to use their previously published or attributed material in this book.

Cover Design   Alejandro Baigorri
Art Direction   Matt Young
Editor   Lia Ottaviano

Printed in the United States of America.

ISBN: 978-0-578-84967-6

table of contents

WELL, HELLO FRIEND.

Sit down. Get comfy. Let's get to know each other.

First, you should know I'm deeply flawed. I'll be the first person to tell you, I don't know everything. I don't know a lot of stuff. Seriously, like most things. I cannot tell you after more than thirty years on this planet which containers can and cannot go safely into a microwave.

I do know that in my many conversations with friends, family, coworkers, acquaintances, and utter strangers, there's a lot of stuff people know but don't talk about. Why are we hiding valuable information from each other, as though navigating through life should be a mysterious secret?

The truth is, we all know different stuff. What we each know—I mean know with certainty—is determined by a ton of different factors: our parents, our teachers, the year we were born, the place we grew up, who our friends were, the TV shows we watched, our bullies, and thousands of other things. We all had different upbringings, and so we all have different information. I can only promise you one thing: everyone has a gap in knowledge. Grown-ups taught us from what they knew but technological advancements, a rapidly changing society, and those grown-ups' own upbringings made it impossible for them to teach us everything.

That's where this book comes in. It's packed with lots of lessons we never learned. This book isn't going to teach you how to post the best selfie, select the best dairy alternative, or craft an incredible breakup text. This is practical life shit, in one spot. That's it.

Not everything in this book is for everyone. That's why I wrote it in short, easy-to-digest chapters. If something doesn't apply to you, skip it. I'm not your mother. I won't check up on you to make sure you did your homework.

We'll start with the *really* practical stuff: career and money shit. It's the boring, logical stuff that we need to talk about before we move into the sections on heart and soul. If you've already got the practical stuff on lock, skip the whole first section. Put the book on a shelf and come back to certain chapters as you need them in your life. You won't need everything today, this month, or even this year.

Following career and money shit, you'll find three more sections: relationship shit, mind shit, and life shit. Those sections urge you to dig deeper into your mind and heart until you reach the core: how to make this crazy life journey as awesome as possible without going completely batshit crazy.

This is, essentially, a memoir disguised as a self-help book. You're going to learn a ton of shit through my failures. I share personal anecdotes here—some of you will likely judge them. Go for it. I doubt you're more critical of me than I am of myself. What can I say: I've made some mistakes.

My entire goal is to help anyone out there who's struggling. This book is for those of you who have spent hours digging through Google search results only to come up empty handed, and more confused than you were when you started. It's for those of you who don't even know what to Google in the first place. This book is for all the conversations you didn't even know you should be having, and all the conversations you were too afraid to have. This book is for those of you who are just trying to grow the fuck up... gracefully.

Oh yeah, and there will be profanity.

PART ONE

CAREER & MONEY SHIT

HAVE SAVINGS

How old were you when you learned there were savings accounts that could make you a bunch of money for free? Literally, no extra money *from* you, but lots of extra money *for* you. Was it today? Were you today-years-old? It's okay, you can tell me.

I'm not talking about those big banks with all their fancy buildings on every street corner. Sure, the lollipops are nice, but their interest rates aren't. I'm talking about high yield savings accounts. You can typically find them online, which means you don't even have to put on pants to sign up for one.

I think it's safe to say that we all understood the concept of savings at one point or another leading up to adulthood. The issue is, for most of us, no one ever taught us an easy, practical way to save. We were always taught to "save for the future" or "put away money for a rainy day." That's all good advice, but saving money was easier for a generation that didn't have a major recession and a pandemic in their early years of adulthood.

Let's think about this practically.

You get your first job. Congratulations! Let's say your salary is $30,000 a year. An employee earning $30,000 a year, paid bi-weekly, usually earns $1,153.85 gross pay per check, or roughly $576 a week. Typically, when you get set up with a new company, they ask for your direct deposit information. Give them two accounts. The first account will be your savings account, where you'll deposit a small amount of each paycheck— let's say $25 - $50. Then, arrange for the remaining amount to go to your main bank account. If direct deposit isn't an option at work, set up an automatic transfer once or twice a month from your main checking account to your savings account. Think of it like a bill you're paying, only the money is being paid to your future self.

Do this on day one of the job. If you make this arrangement from your first paycheck, you'll never even notice the money's missing. You'll never feel like you're getting paid less than what you usually do, because you'll always receive your standard paycheck amount. If you put $50 away every paycheck, that's $100 a month.

I know. Oof. $100 a month sounds like a lot when you're only making a little more than $2,300 a month. I like to think of this as a happiness tax. You're paying for it now, like you would any other taxes, but much like a refund at the end of the year, you'll receive back future happiness and financial security.

When you get a raise, say from $30,000 a year to $35,000 a year, maybe you increase your savings amount from $50 to $100 per paycheck. Again, you won't notice the new amount is missing because you never saw it in your bank account to begin with. Plus, a $5,000 increase is almost $200 more per paycheck, so an extra $50 won't feel like much. Your main account will see a $150 increase per paycheck regardless.

Every time you get a raise, double your contribution, or at least raise it substantially, if doubling isn't possible within your budget. Even increasing your contribution from $100 to $175 (vs. $200) is substantial. Every time you get a birthday check from your grandmother, a bonus, win the lottery, or receive money you didn't see coming, add it to the savings account. Free money and unexpected earnings are always wonderful; they're even better when they make more money over time.

Next up is picking the right account. I recommend a high yield savings account that's online only. A high yield savings account will typically provide anywhere from 0.5% - 2.5% interest depending on the current economy and the bank's individual rate. Google "online high yield savings account" and compare various banks. Double-check their track record and reviews in addition to their interest rate. Just because they are offering 2% when everyone else is offering 1.8% doesn't mean they're the best, most-well liked option—it just means they're the highest one.

So, what does 2% interest really mean? That means if you put $1,000 in an account with 2% interest, it will make $20 a year just for sitting in there.

Now that we've covered the basics, I'm going to throw some radical ideas at you that have worked for me.

Your savings account should not be attached to your checking account. They shouldn't even be within the same bank. It's hard when you're beginning your savings journey to not touch the money. Trust me. Having a little extra money makes pretty things in fancy stores look prettier.

Some accounts will send you a debit card when you open the account—cut it up when it arrives. I told you these were radical ideas—but trust me. If you cut it up, you won't be tempted to use it on a whim. You can connect your savings account to your main bank account for deposits and withdrawals, but most of these transfers will take about three to five business days to complete. That sounds like a long time, but honestly, it's a blessing. You can't impulse spend this money. If you want to spend it, you have to think about it for a few days. Or at the very least, you have to put in the effort to transfer it knowing it will take a few days, which will make you really evaluate if this purchase or expense is worth it.

When my car broke down, I knew I would need to find a new car in the next week or so. I immediately transferred the amount I would be willing to spend on a down payment, $5,000, into my checking account. I did this mostly because I don't trust myself around shiny objects. I knew if I found a beautiful, fancy, expensive car that needed an $8,000 down payment, I might spend the money and then regret it later when I needed that money for something else. By transferring $5,000, I knew my budget and had to stick to it. It also made my negotiations at car dealerships easier because I could tell dealers the exact number I was putting down and the exact number I wanted to spend monthly and let them figure out how to sell me the car I wanted. It's amazing how being firm on numbers can make negotiations a bit more flexible.

A fun bonus of saving money is that you get weirdly excited when your savings start going up. When I hit milestones—$5,000, $10,000, $30,000—saving money became addictive. I didn't want to see my savings go down, so I adjusted my monthly budget to make sure I didn't have to dip into my savings and second-guessed purchases I would've otherwise bought. Sorry life-sized Ryan Gosling cardboard cutout, you just weren't worth it.

Once I started saving, I stopped making life decisions based on fear. I no longer took a job because it seemed like the "right financial" choice. I knew I had money to fall back on so I would take the risk and choose a job that might be better for my career in the long term rather than my bank account in the short term.

Money doesn't buy happiness, but it does buy choices. If I save $800 a month for a year and lose my job unexpectedly, I have money for my $1,600 per month rent for a few months. I now have the choice of what to do next rather than taking a job out of necessity.

I no longer have to choose between an amazing vacation and making rent because I know I can afford both, even if I have to borrow some money from my savings. While I try not to use my savings for vacations, having the money there lets me take the trips I want knowing I have a safety net.

If you picked up this book looking for some guidance on self-love and improved well-being, start here. It's not yoga or meditation, but having savings is self-love, too. It gives you peace of mind, and is there anything more calming than that?

Give It A Fucking Shot

- ☐ Google "high yield savings accounts".

- ☐ Find an online bank with a good interest rate and open an account.

- ☐ Change your direct deposit at work to allow a set amount or a percentage of your paycheck to go into your savings account. If you don't have direct deposit, set up an automatic transfer.

- ☐ Don't touch the money in savings for at least six to twelve months. This will give you time to see it grow and prove to yourself that you don't need it.

"MY DEAR FELLOW, WHO WILL LET YOU?"

"THAT'S NOT THE POINT. THE POINT IS, WHO WILL STOP ME?"

— AYN RAND, *THE FOUNTAINHEAD*

PLAN FOR RETIREMENT EARLY

I'm in my thirties and retirement feels like a distant dream, as tangible as flying cars and colonizing Mars. Unfortunately, retirement is something I have to plan for, as it's inevitable (unlike the other two things, which would be awesome but may not actually happen in my lifetime—get on it, Elon).

When I was first offered a 401(k) at my second job ever, I was a naïve twenty-three-year-old who didn't even understand how to approach it. I understood that it was money taken out before taxes and put away in an account I didn't get to touch until I was older. I didn't see why I needed one, though. I'm going to have savings, social security, and an insanely huge mansion I can sell when I retire and make a ton of money from. Why would I need to put away 5% of my paycheck for my future self?

Because none of the other things are guaranteed. Social security could run out, I may have a medical problem or an unplanned life event that eats up all of my savings, and while I fully believe my dream of living in a giant mansion with an Olympic-size pool will one day be a reality, I have to admit that it may not make it beyond my fantasy world.

I graduated college in 2010, right after the 2008 recession. I heard stories of my classmates' parents losing huge portions of their retirement savings. At the time of my graduation, we were still in the depths of a very slow economic recovery. 401(k)s hit the floor faster than me trying to slam dunk a basketball, but what no one told me was that within a few years, everything would rebound and be even better than it was before the crash. I thought, "Why would I ever consider putting money into something that could be cut in half in one day?" The truth is that if you don't, you'll spend your retirement eating microwave dinners like a broke college kid.

So, how do we invest in a 401(k) without it affecting our broke, young lives? We want to make sure our future is secure while still enjoying bottomless mimosa brunches.

By using the same strategy we used for savings. First, if your company matches your 401(k) contributions, do whatever you have to do to get their matching contribution. It's free money. You would never turn away $5 from someone offering it to you with no strings attached, so why would you turn away money from your company? If they say, "If you deposit 5% or more from each paycheck into your 401(k), then we will match 2%," do it. That's basically a 2% raise without having to sit in an awkward negotiation meeting (don't worry; we'll get to that).

If your company doesn't have a matching 401(k) policy, and many don't anymore, then do it for yourself. Figure out how much you could put away without impacting your life and do that. Treat it the same way you treated the savings account. Pick a percentage or dollar amount you're comfortable with on day one of the job, and you'll never see your paycheck change and never miss the money. Every time you get a raise, add another 1-2%.

If you don't work for a company that offers a 401(k), no worries. You can open an IRA. They're similar in nature and will help you save in a similar fashion. A 401(k) is connected to a company while an IRA is connected to you, regardless of where you work.

Got it? Cool.

Next up, the fun shit—elections. Not presidential. Electing who to give your money to is way easier than voting for the next leader of our country. First, you have to pick stuff to invest in with your 401(k) or IRA money. The most common type of funds offered in these plans are mutual or index funds (I'll get into this in more detail soon). Some 401(k)s offer a bond fund or a foreign fund, but they're usually more limited options than the mutual funds. What

I recommend is that you look into the funds offered by your plan and Google them to find out which ones have done well over the past three to five years. Look for funds that have gone up steadily: for example, at a 10% return each year. If they've got a history of highs and lows but have returned a higher amount, like 25%, last year, it might be worth the risk if you're young enough not to mind the drama.

There's a ton of information on the Internet. Google what you don't know but don't use not knowing something as an excuse. When you reach fifty and realize you only have ten years to save, you're going to be super pissed at yourself for not doing it sooner. Playing catch up is so much harder than playing the long game. Ever try to race someone who started half a mile ahead of you?

Words to Know

ROTH ACCOUNT
You pay taxes now, so you don't pay them later. Basically, if you put in $100 to your 401(k) account from your paycheck, your 401(k) account will only reflect the amount of $100 *minus* taxes—for example, $85. However, when you take the money out after you retire, you won't pay taxes on it—you'll get the whole $85. And at the rate of inflation, who knows how much taxes will be at that far away time.

TRADITIONAL ACCOUNT
You don't pay any taxes on your deposits. If you put in $100, your 401(k) account will reflect the entire $100. This does mean, however, that when you retire and withdraw the money, taxes will be taken out then.

PRE-TAX
You may notice that some 401(k) deductions are taken from your paycheck pre-tax. Money is deducted from your paycheck before

federal, state, and local taxes are taken out. Let's say your standard paycheck is $2,300 gross. After taxes, deductions and all that jazz, you receive a check for $1900. Your $100 contribution is taken from the $2,300 amount, not the $1,900 amount. This means that if you deposit $100 into your 401(k), you may notice your paycheck is only about $80 or so less than usual. That's because the $100 was taken out before the other deductions.

401(K) VS. IRA

Basically, a 401(k) is something your employer or company sets up for you. An IRA is something you set up for yourself. They are run in a similar manner, except the 401(k) is linked to your company and an IRA is basically a bank account you set up for yourself—that you can't touch until your hair turns gray and you have a sufficient amount of crows' feet. Think of it like a self-established trust fund. 401(k) accounts are employer-sponsored, so your employer would have to offer one for you to be eligible. If that isn't an option for any number of reasons, look into an IRA. If you're self-employed, an independent contractor, or even a part-time employee not eligible for company benefits, an IRA is likely your best bet.

PREMATURE DISTRIBUTIONS

This has a lot of fancy synonyms, such as "early withdrawal," but "premature distributions" means that if you take out the money before you turn 59 ½ (I know, super specific), you get fined and taxed and you lose a bunch of your money. I'm not saying don't do it; do it if you absolutely have to. But this should be a last resort for getting money. You're basically losing money you worked so hard for and paying the banks to access your own money. You're better off taking money from a savings account, stock portfolio, or even a loan if it makes sense interest-wise before you take money out early from a retirement account.

MUTUAL OR INDEX FUNDS

Mutual funds and index funds are super similar. They're practically synonyms for one another. They are comprised of various stocks or bonds that make up one fund. For example, S&P 500 Index Fund is a fund made up of the largest publicly traded companies in the U.S. (like Apple and Amazon). They take a bunch of stocks or bonds and bundle them into one neat and tidy fund. The main difference between them is index funds are passively managed while mutual funds are actively managed by fancy stock-picking people. Mutual funds have a higher fee because those fancy stock-picking people like to get paid.

LARGE CAP, MID-CAP, AND SMALL CAP

Large cap are the least risky funds but also will likely make you slightly less money than the others. In many cases, they're the safe, sensible choice. Large cap funds are made up of large companies (the ones worth billions). AB Large-Cap Growth Fund, for example, includes companies like Microsoft and Facebook. Mid-cap funds are one step closer towards the risky zone and are between large and small cap funds. Taylor Frigon Core Growth Fund is a mid-cap fund with companies like Wix and Carvana. Small cap funds are the riskier, bad boy alternative but also give you the chance to make more money. The Vanguard Small Cap Index Fund, for example, includes companies like Etsy. Think of it like roulette. A large cap is betting red or black. A mid-cap is betting columns. A small cap is betting numbers. If you're young, like in your twenties, and don't mind the risk (let's face it, we like to be a bit dramatic when we're young), maybe choose a small cap. If you're closer to retirement, a large cap might make the most sense.

Give It A Fucking Shot

- [ ] First, stop freaking out. It's going to be fine. Just walk into your HR office tomorrow and ask them how to get set up with a 401(k).

- [ ] If you're a freelancer, independent contractor, part time employee, or don't have a job with a 401(k) option, also stop freaking out and look into your IRA options. They're structured similarly but you're fully in charge of them.

- [ ] Then, pick out some funds you want to contribute to. Give it about an hour or so of Googling—max. Don't overthink it, but don't blindly pick funds.

- [ ] Sit back and watch yourself make money that 59½-year-old you will appreciate. Maybe by then you can buy a flying car with it.

INVEST

When I used to hear the word invest, my mind conjured up images of men in suits on Wall Street and words like "hedge fund manager" and "acquisitions." Guess what? That's fancy investing. There's also super un-fancy investing. What no one told me is that investing is just company-regulated gambling.

There are a lot of apps out there that can help you invest, like Robinhood, Acorns, or Fidelity. You can do it passively or actively. You can invest $20 or $20,000. It's entirely up to you.

You can have an app invest spare change for you (like Acorns). Just link it to your checking account and they'll take care of the rest.

Or you can find ways to invest that are slightly more active (like Robinhood). When I started investing, I had been given a $1,000 bonus and decided I was going to try to invest it somewhere. Hey, free money. Why not risk it all? I did some Googling and found a few utility ETFs (I'll explain what that is soon) which seemed super safe. I put half of my money there. Then I found some stocks whose ticker names I found funny, like NUGT (a gold ETF) and HA (Hawaiian Airlines), and put half of my money there. I figured if I lost it all, then I spent $1,000 on a fun experience, just like gambling. At least I would learn how to invest. Do I recommend you do it the same way I did? Not necessarily, but it made investing for me more fun.

Before we move on, let's discuss some of the fancy words you need to know to get started.

Words to Know

STOCKS

This is an investment in one company. Let's say you invest in the company that makes your phone. You like your phone and you think they'll continue to make better versions that people will like. You now have stock in a technology company.

ETFS

This is an investment of multiple companies at once. Let's say you like your phone but you also like your friend's phone, your neighbor's phone, and your mom's phone. You really don't know which phone company is the best. You can invest in an ETF (exchange-traded fund) which is a single fund made up of a bunch of companies. ETFs are similar to mutual or index funds in structure (they're multiple companies in one) but act more like stocks in their day-to-day activity (they go up and down throughout the day). Maybe you find a technology ETF that consists of ten different technology companies. Now you can invest in all of the phone companies at once, just by purchasing one ETF. Just because the ETF is made up of multiple companies doesn't mean it costs more than a traditional stock. You're investing a little into multiple companies so the cost per company will be less than if you bought stock in each company individually. It's kind of like buying a travel set of toiletries. If you buy a set of travel toiletries for $10, it could include tiny shampoo, tiny conditioner, tiny body wash, and tiny lotion. If you bought all four of those items at full-size, it would cost way more than $10, but this way you get a little sample of each without fully committing. If you need only shampoo, you might just buy a full-sized shampoo instead.

STOCKS VS. ETFS

If you're super passionate about a company, invest in them. Go all in. Buy the full-sized shampoo. If you aren't sure, play the field a bit and invest in an ETF. ETFs tend to be less volatile. Let's use the same example. Say you pick an ETF that has ten technology companies, each holding an equal 10% stake in the ETF. If one of the ten technology stocks completely fails, only 10% of that ETF is falling. I've found that in a time where scandals are happening daily—if the CEO of a company does something stupid—a stock could fall hard but an ETF might just stumble. The flip side of that is if a stock does extremely well, then the ETF only sees a marginal benefit reflected within that 10%, whereas the people who invested purely in that stock are rolling in money now.

SHARES

A company is worth $X. When you buy a share, you own that much of that company. Maybe Company A is worth $1,000,000 and they are selling shares for $10 each. You buy a share and now own $1/100,000^{th}$ of that company. For our world, shares are collectively known as "stock." Saying, "I have stock in that company," really means, "I own some shares."

INVESTMENT PORTFOLIO

Say you own three shares of stock in a technology company, four shares in a pharmaceutical company, and one share of a gold ETF (yes, you can literally invest in companies that sell gold—remember NUGT?). Congratulations—that's your portfolio. Your portfolio is made up of three different investments.

LIMIT SELLS AND LIMIT BUYS

This is what I call lazy trading. Let's say I really love the company that makes my phone but they're currently selling at $40 a share. That's too steep for my wallet right now, but I see that a month ago they were selling for $32 a share and that definitely works for me. I can set a limit buy, through apps such as Robinhood, that are good for 90 days and say, "If this stock ever dips below $32, buy it." The same is true for selling a stock. Sometimes you want to offload a stock but don't feel like checking daily to see if it's the right time to sell. If you bought a stock at $40 a share and since then, it's been down at $32 - $35, you can say "If this stock ever goes above $50, sell it." That's a limit sell (and a $10 profit—good work).

Now that you've gotten some terms down and you're ready to go full-blown Wolf of Wall Street, let's talk through some nitty-gritty aspects of investing. Always check fees. Sometimes you get fined when you withdraw; sometimes you get fined if you choose international instead of domestic stock. Just read the fine print and double check. The fees usually aren't major, but it's always worth checking. If you can find a company that doesn't fine you to invest, go with them over someone who does charge you to invest. It might mean a little extra legwork on your end, but you're prepared now. You've got this.

Don't check that shit every day. You'll drive yourself mad. The market fluctuates and if you're going to check it daily, you'll see that today you lost $7 and yesterday you gained $18 but on Monday you lost $40. Stop. Check it every now and then to just see how you are doing overall.

Do your research before investing in a company. You're trusting these companies with your money, so make sure you like what the company stands for just as much as you like how much money they could potentially make you.

You're smart, so invest wisely. Don't invest more money than you can afford and choose the funds you think will be best for you.

So go on. Give it a fucking shot.

BUY A CAR

No one talks about how hard it is to buy a car, but everyone talks about how easy it could be. There's a car commercial on every five minutes advertising $0 down and no payments for your first three months—but no one ever talks about the practical, straightforward way to buy a car.

First of all, it's the 21st century. Go online and do some research. Autotrader, Edmunds, and Cars.com are all awesome places to start.

Consider the specs you want but don't get crazy. How important is horsepower going to be when you spend most of your time in the car going to and from the grocery store? Think pragmatically—if you have a long commute, do you want your car to be comfortable and have a good sound system? If you do a lot of city driving, do you want your car to have a parking assistant or backup camera? If you camp or go on road trips, how important is a roof rack or trunk storage?

For me, I wanted a hybrid so I could save money on gas, a navigation system to get around in the city, and leather seats so it was easy to clean out dog hair from my many dog-accompanied road trips. I narrowed down my options from all of the available cars in the universe to four cars I liked. I found an auto mall with dealerships for all four of those car brands and went one day to test drive them all. Then I walked away without a car.

Why? First, I wanted to think about which one I really liked the best, not which one had the best salesman or snacks in the lobby. Also, I wanted to shop for my first choice online to make sure I got the best deal. If I could get the same car for less money at a dealership ten miles down the road, I wanted to know.

Even though I knew that out of the four cars I test drove I liked the Lexus best, while I was sitting in the dealership, I scrolled through other dealer listings for the same car and noticed this particular dealership was asking about $5k above average. No, thank you. I went home and spent the next few days searching for that exact car, with leather seats and navigation, within 100 miles. I soon found one for the price I wanted. Since I had already test driven the car, I knew I liked it. I called the dealership, asked if they could hold it for me, drove over the next day, and bought it.

In the twenty-four hours between when I found the car and when I bought it, I called my insurance to see how much my rate would go up, I double checked my budget to make sure it would fit, and I called my usual mechanic to ask him if he thought this was a good, reliable car to buy. When all checked out positively, I felt confident before I even walked in the door.

Next up—the negotiation. There is always room for one, even when they say it's a fixed price. If you have a trade in, negotiate that. Get quotes from sites like CarMax and Carvana, and use those rates to get the best trade-in deal you can. If the dealership shows you the monthly payment and it seems higher than you thought it would be, ask for an itemized breakdown of where those additional fees are coming from. "You said the car was $20,000 with all taxes and fees included over sixty months, but that should be $333/month and you're saying it'll be $360/month. Where's the extra $27 coming from? Is it interest? Can I see a breakdown of it?" Chances are they hid some fees, and even the request to get an itemized breakdown might make some of those fees go away.

If you're buying a brand-spanking-new car and have a bit of spare time on your hands, go to half a dozen different dealerships for that car and ask for their best offer on paper. Then walk away. Say you're buying a Honda Civic. Walk into Honda dealership A and say, "What's your best deal on this car?". Then get a printed copy of the deal and leave. Walk to Honda dealership B and say, "Dealership A offered me this, can you beat it?". Once you get their offer, go to dealership C, show them the better of the two, and ask if they can beat it. Keep doing this until you hit a number you like. Then go back to your contacts at the other dealerships and see if they will beat your final offer. This will take a bit of time, but you could end up saving thousands of dollars.

Lastly, don't accept any dealership's interest rate because they say it's the best. When I purchased my car, I researched some credit unions via NCUA.gov and filled out an online application to one that offered me an interest rate under 3%. When I went to the dealership the next day, they tried to give me a 5.4% interest rate, to which I said, "No, thank you," and got all the paperwork from them that I needed to give to the credit union. You don't have to go with the dealership's bank; you just have to get a loan independently within about five days of buying the car.

Another super weird tip that's often overlooked is thinking about sales tax. If you live in or near a city, you may have higher sales tax than surrounding areas an hour or two away. I wouldn't recommend leaving the state, because then you have to deal with registration transfers and extra paperwork hassle. I live in Los Angeles, which has a 9.75% sales tax when factoring in state, county, and city taxes. In Orange County, about one hour away, the sales tax is 7.75% for all state and local taxes. If you're buying a $20,000 car, a one-hour drive can save you $400. That may not seem like a lot but think about it this way: that's over one month of payments.

One last strange tip: If you can, put some of your down payment on a credit card that you'll pay off immediately. During my most recent car purchase, the dealership let me put $5,000 down on my credit card, which I paid off two days later once it posted to the account. My credit card's rewards program gave me over $200 in cash back on that $5,000 charge.

Give It A Fucking Shot

- ☐ Google your specs and narrow down your choices to less than six cars.

- ☐ Test drive those cars but do *not* buy that day.

- ☐ Find your top choice online for the best rate possible. Don't be afraid to travel an hour or two to save a few thousand dollars.

- ☐ Transfer the amount you want for a down payment to your checking account.

- ☐ Call your car insurance and get a quote for your new rate. If it's too high, shop around for new insurance before giving up on that car.

- ☐ Call a trusted source or read Google reviews of your top choice.

- ☐ Fill out some preliminary applications with credit unions to see what rate you can get for a loan.

- ☐ Get quotes from used-car retailers like CarMax or Carvana to estimate your trade-in value. You can do this through their website, without having to go in person.

- ☐ Go in loaded with information and get the best deal you can.

CONSIDER A SIDE HUSTLE

The grown-ups in the generation above us made it seem like you'd find something you're insanely passionate about and do that forever. If that's you, amazing. If that's you and you still can't manage to afford your bills, that's normal. Everyone is good at multiple things. Just because you have one thing that you do for work doesn't mean it has to be the only thing you do. Maybe your day job is what pays the bills while you have freelance gigs on the side that ignite your passion. Or your day job is what you're passionate about, but you want some extra cash to build up a savings account or roll around in. Whatever the reason is, side hustles are becoming the norm for many.

Having a side hustle doesn't mean working two full-time jobs. Don't stretch yourself so thin that you no longer enjoy life. Side hustling just means finding something that can bring in a little extra cash flow. This could be writing articles for a website that pays per article. It could be babysitting some nights or weekends. It could be walking dogs or driving for a ridesharing company in your free time.

I first moved to Los Angeles to pursue acting. I was working a day job in production to pay bills, but that quickly turned into fifty-plus-hour weeks. One day I was talking to my acting teacher about my day job and saying that it was great to have this work, especially in the same field I'm pursuing with acting, but the days were feeling very long. He mentioned that I could be a waiter and work half as much for the same amount of money. I thought about it for a while but decided to stick with my bill-paying day job, and I'm so thankful I did. It grew into a full-blown career and now I'm making more money than I ever could have as a waiter. Waiting tables would have been great short term, but choosing a day job that fueled my side hustle benefitted both my wallet and my passion and kept me motivated.

The key is to choose the side hustle that's right for you. There are passive income side hustles and active income side hustles. Passive income hustles usually take a lot of time up front and then bring in income with little to no work over time. An example of this on a big scale is purchasing and renovating a house and then renting it out. The work comes at the beginning but you make money from renters over time. An example of this on a smaller scale is creating a cross-stitch pattern that you sell on Etsy that brings in small amounts of money over time.

Active income hustles are endeavors that require your time, like dog walking, delivering food, and babysitting. These are the types of hustles that need little set up and are typically flexible in terms of when you can do them, but they also demand some of your time to complete, as opposed to being automated.

Here are some additional active side hustle ideas:

- Write articles for websites as a freelancer.
- Edit videos (wedding videos, acting reels, birthday celebrations).
- Create and edit cover letters and resumes.
- Be a virtual assistant.
- Start a dog walking business.
- Become a delivery driver.
- Tutor online.
- Find one-off gigs on websites like Upwork or Fiverr.

Here are some additional passive side hustle ideas:

- Manage a rental property.
- Create downloadable art that you can sell for prints or clothing patches.

- Design a class that can be made available through an online course website.
- Develop an app or software people can download.
- Create a font and sell it online.
- Purchase a few website domain names to sell later.

Give It A Fucking Shot

- ☐ Make a list of a few things you would consider for a side hustle.

- ☐ Create a plan and timeline for getting those things off the ground.

- ☐ Launch them and enjoy the extra income.

NEGOTIATE YOUR SALARY

Have you ever been asked about your salary expectations in a job interview? How quickly did you sweat through your shirt?

It's sometimes hard to figure out how much money you should ask for. If you interview for a dream job and they ask about your salary, you may have a slight moment of panic. That's totally normal. For me, I typically throw out a range. If you can, do research before the interview on websites like Glassdoor or LinkedIn to find out an average salary range so you aren't thrown off by the question.

Don't tell them what you're currently making. At the time of publication, over half of U.S states have banned employers from asking for prospective employees' current salary. Even if it isn't illegal, it doesn't matter. You're currently doing one job, and if you take this new job, you'll be doing that job. The only thing that should matter is the salary for the new job.

Prospective employers ask for your current salary to implement a method called "anchoring." Once a number has been thrown out into the universe, you're anchored to that number. Say you're looking to make $80,000, but when they ask what you're currently making, you say $50,000. Now you're anchored to the number $50,000, so asking for $80,000 may seem like a large leap. If they ask what you're currently making, you can pivot to say, "Well, for this type of position, I'd expect my salary range to be $75,000 to $85,000." This gets you closer to where you want to be by "anchoring" you into $75,000. You may also choose to have the range be $80,000 to $90,000 so you have some room to negotiate above $80,000. You may land closer to $82,000 or $83,000 with that method, but you run the risk of them thinking you're too expensive with a base of $80,000. That's why you should do the research before you go in to find out the average range for X type of role at X type of company.

If you aren't sure how to answer the question in terms of salary range, ask a few more questions about responsibility, room for growth, and benefits.

If your prospective employer tells you that the salary isn't negotiable, something else must be. If they offer two weeks' vacation, you can say something like, "I understand the salary amount is locked. Would you be willing to negotiate paid leave?" If you want immediate healthcare options, try, "It's my understanding that the benefits do not take effect until after 90 days of employment. If I sign the contract by end of day, would you consider waiving the probation period to allow benefits to begin immediately?"

Never take the first offer. Even if you don't feel comfortable with the fixed amount, there are ways to feel like you came out ahead. You could get an extra week of vacation, a better parking space, a matching 401(k), an expense account, or even a relocation package. There are plenty of items on the table beyond your rate of pay.

Give It A Fucking Shot

☐ Research the average salary for the position for which you're interviewing. Consider your location, your experience, the size of the company, and the particulars of the position.

☐ Decide your salary range ahead of time.

☐ Plan to be flexible but know what is non-negotiable to you. If you won't take this job for less than $X, be prepared to walk away.

☐ See the *Stop Talking So Much* section for more advice.

NEGOTIATE YOUR RAISE

You want to know a weird fact about the world? No one wants to just give you money. I guess I had this idea in my head that when I got out of high school, college, whatever, I would get a job with a salary and then every year or so they'd give me more money. Nope. No one wants to give out money.

So, we have to ask for raises. For every math class I took in school, somehow this was never covered. I took multiple years of algebra classes, but the public education system skipped Make More Money classes. There are a hundred great ways to ask for a raise. There are also a hundred ways to definitely not ask for a raise. Let's review a couple of both.

First, remember you work for a company. Even if it's just you and one other person, you work for a company. This is business. This isn't personal. You can be the most amazing human ever, but the raise is dependent on what you offer to the company and what the company can offer you.

Next, nothing is owed to you. You don't get a raise because you worked there ten years. You don't get a raise because the company made more money this year than last year. You don't get a raise because the person sitting next to you got one.

Again, this is a business. It's a machine. How did you help the machine?

That's where we begin. Before you go into the meeting, gather data to support the argument that you've added value to the company. Did you land four new clients for the company this month? Did you switch the company to a new software that saves them $10,000 a year? Did you absorb new duties, previously held by another position that was never replaced? Did you train other employees? Did you streamline any protocols that save people time, therefore saving the company money? You get the idea.

Next, is there an outline in your contract that states when reviews are scheduled? Does it say every year? Every six months? If so, ask for a review as you approach this date. Your company may schedule a review for you, but some may hope you forget and don't reach out. If there is no previously specified time frame, ask for a review after a reasonable amount of time with the company.

When the meeting time comes, prepare, prepare, prepare. Prepare like you would for a job interview or tea with the Queen of England. Know your strengths and flaunt them. Know your weaknesses, and if asked, acknowledge the work you'll put in to fixing them. Most importantly, know your value.

What you don't want to mention are things like, "I just bought a new car and need more money to pay for it," or, "I have a baby coming and I hear those are expensive," or, "Joe just got a raise and I didn't." Focus on you and what you mean to the company. Remind them they're lucky to have you. Your new car isn't your boss's problem. The new baby likely means they'll get less access to you. And Joe's raise has nothing to do with your success.

It's okay if the entire conversation is about you and your accomplishments within the company and money doesn't come up. They may have to check with other people before approving a raise. They may be waiting for a quarter to close, or a sales projection report. There are other factors at work, so just be sure to follow up a few days later if you don't hear from them.

If they return with a number that's lower than you expected, ask if the raise is negotiable or if there is an opportunity to revisit this rate in a few months.

Give It A Fucking Shot

- ☐ Ask HR or your supervisor for a review meeting.

- ☐ In the days leading up to the meeting, begin to think about and write down the ways you've contributed to the company. Print out the list and bring it with you.

- ☐ Prepare for the meeting. Know your strengths, know your weaknesses, and go in ready to speak towards them.

- ☐ If you don't hear back about a raise within a week from the meeting, follow up with your supervisor.

- ☐ See the *Stop Talking So Much* section for more advice.

"THE GOAL ISN'T MORE MONEY. THE GOAL IS LIVING LIFE ON YOUR TERMS."

— CHRIS BROGAN

NEVER MAKE A DECISION BECAUSE OF MONEY

When I took my first job, I didn't even know the salary until I had already said yes. That was stupid. I didn't get a chance to negotiate my rate because I was too busy celebrating that someone wanted to pay me. But it taught me something valuable. Never make a decision because of money.

Up to this moment, we've been talking about how to make you money. Don't get me wrong—I want your bank account to be so fucking loaded you don't know what to do with it all. But making money is very different than letting the concept of making money run your life. Yes, money is important. But the problem with it being a factor in the decision-making process is that it can carry more weight than other things.

There were bus benches in my neighborhood in the early 2000s that said, "What would you do if money wasn't a factor?" The phrase was probably a marketing tool for a bank, or the lottery, or something—I have no idea—but that particular question still intrigues me. What decisions would you make if you didn't factor in money?

Imagine you make a pros and cons list for a new job. You may weigh the benefits of a promotion in title, an easier commute, and a more creative workload, but if they want you to take a 2% pay cut, you may not take it. There are times in your life when a 2% pay cut isn't possible given your current circumstances and that's always valid. On the flip side, you may choose to stay at a job that's stagnant and less creative because of the money. You could be setting yourself back in your career overall due to a shortsighted monetary decision.

Once, I was offered a job that paid $15k more than my current one, but the company was twice as far, which meant doubling my commute. It wasn't really a promotion, but rather the same job I already had at a different company. The company was a brand-new startup, which meant a higher risk of failure and future unemployment, and they didn't offer health insurance, which meant I'd have to get my own or go uninsured. I decided not to take it and to wait for something better. Had I looked at it objectively, not taking it would have been a no-brainer, but the money got in my head and made me consider accepting it for longer than I should have.

If you're facing a tough choice, try taking money out of your decision-making process. Instead, factor in your future happiness and give that the weight it deserves. Yes, it sounds corny and I'm even cringing a little while writing it, but it's true. We frequently push our happiness aside to make a few dollars. This time, push money aside to make a happier you.

Give It A Fucking Shot

☐ When facing a tough decision, write out a list of pros and cons, but do not put money anywhere on it. See where you land before money factors in.

☐ Try envisioning your life five years from now. Still keeping money aside, does the decision at hand make sense for the five-years-from-now you?

HAVE CREDIT PROTECTION

A number of years ago, there was a data breach at one of the three major consumer credit reporting databases. I went on a website that lets you know whether or not your information had been stolen and lo and behold, there I was. I felt so violated. Someone out there was catfishing companies, pretending to be me, and making me look bad.

Within a few months I was being mailed declined credit applications for Kay Jewelers and Sprint. It was scary to have my information out there. Who were these people pretending to be me? It was also a little insulting that these people didn't think I had Harry Winston or Tiffany's level credit. I didn't, but it hurt that they didn't try to aim a little higher.

After receiving my third declined credit application in the span of only a few weeks, I decided to lock my credit and file a police report.

It wasn't until this whole ordeal that I learned you could lock your own credit for free anytime. Like the Trojan condom ads said in the 90s, it "helps reduce the risk." Of course, they were talking about a different kind of protection, but the concept remains the same. Protection is cool, even when it's protecting yourself from identity theft.

Side note: it's super easy.

The main three credit bureaus in the United States are Equifax, Experian, and TransUnion. If you go on each of their websites and search to either "freeze" or "lock" your credit, they'll walk you through the steps on how to do so. There's a fourth one I locked called Innovis.

It's smaller and less popular, but apparently hackers don't care about the size of the credit bureau when stealing your information.

It takes five minutes to lock your credit. All you need is your address, your social security number, and to answer a few security questions. Then, voila, your credit is locked. If you ever apply for a credit card, car loan, or mortgage, you can go onto each of the above-mentioned websites and request a temporary unlock. Just set the dates you want your credit unlocked and relocked, and it will happen automatically.

When your credit is locked, no one, including you, can open anything requiring your social security number. This includes opening credit cards, applying for leases or mortgages, and acquiring an automotive loan. Nothing. This protects you from identity theft and is completely free.

Many major credit card companies also offer free credit monitoring so you can see if anyone has recently attempted to use your information. Just log in to your online credit card account and see if they offer FICO protection or credit monitoring. My Discover and Capital One cards both offer it for free, and I get an email monthly telling me if anyone tried to open an account using my information (even if they failed).

Undoing the damage from stolen credit can take years, even decades. It could ruin your chances at getting a home mortgage, car loan or even student loan.

So get on it. Take some tips from *Home Alone* and set up digital booby traps, Kevin McCallister style. Credit locking and monitoring is easy and stops those identity bandits from stealing your shit.

Give It A Fucking Shot

☐ Spend thirty minutes and lock your credit on all four credit bureau websites. You'll need your social security number to do so.

☐ Save your "unlock" pin from each company in a safe space for when you need them. (I save mine to my phone under contacts using the name of an obscure character from a TV show.) Your pin will let you unlock your credit later on.

GET INSURANCE

Whether it's health insurance, car insurance, dental insurance, or life insurance, I'm convinced it's all an insane process meant to drive people mad. It's like they're testing our will to live by making the process of getting insurance as complicated as possible. Why does it fall on us to figure it out on our own? Insurance companies make piles upon piles of money. Let them fight over you.

Let's take car insurance as an example. There are plenty of websites out there that will compare car insurance rates. Try not to give out your phone number, but if you do, know you'll receive a ton of calls for the next week from your new BFFs, Mr. & Mrs. Insurance Agents. Feel free to answer those calls and save money by pitting their rates against each other. If Company A says, "I saw you inquired about a quote," you can say, "Well, I did, but Company B gave me an online quote already and it's 15% lower than the one your company quoted me. Are you willing to beat their rate?" If they want you, they'll lower their rate to win you over.

If you can't figure out how to get a car insurance rate down, take off some of the fancy features like roadside assistance or rental cars. Also try a higher deductible.

The same goes for health insurance. Make a list of what's important to you—for example: low deductible, in-network and out-of-network options, no referrals for specialists. Below we dive into the differences between HMO and PPO, the differences between coinsurance and copay, and more to help you figure out what's right for you.

IN-NETWORK VS OUT-OF-NETWORK

Simply put, if your doctor's in-network with your insurance, it means they're buddies and have a contract together, so your doctor can bill through your insurance for any visits or procedures done. Out-of-network means they're not in business together, so the doctor's office doesn't have to deal with your insurance, they just bill you directly. Then you have to submit it to your insurance for reimbursement if you have out-of-network coverage. Some places will still bill your insurance but this isn't always the case.

HMO (Health Maintenance Organization)

These are usually the cheapest insurance plans available, but you have to use the plan's doctors. If you want to see a specialist, you need a referral from your primary care doctor first. Basically, it's more hoops to jump through and less options, but a cheaper plan. It's like being a kid: you don't have to worry about money as much but there are more rules you have to follow.

PPO (Preferred Provider Organization)

These plans are typically more expensive, but you have a much bigger range of doctors, you can call a specialist directly to make an appointment without asking your primary care doctor for a referral, and you have an easier time, typically, getting procedures approved through pre-authorization. Overall, these plans offer way less hoops to jump through and way more flexibility, but it costs more. With a PPO, you often get out-of-network coverage as well. For example, your plan may cover 80% of any procedure in-network and 40% of any procedure out-of-network.

EPO (Exclusive Provider Organization)

A lot like a PPO, but you can't go out of network. These tend to be cheaper than PPO plans. So, if your doctor is in-network and your insurance company covers 80%, then you're only paying 20%, but if your doctor is out-of-network and you have an EPO, you're basically uninsured with them and you'll pay 100% of the costs. If you live in a big city or have a major insurer, like Aetna or Blue Cross Blue Shield, you're likely fine with an EPO since tons of doctors are in-network with them. I had an Aetna EPO in Los Angeles and they covered over 90% of the doctors within a twenty-mile radius of me. The only one out-of-network doctor was my eye doctor, so I had to pay from my own wallet anytime I saw him.

COINSURANCE PLAN

This is typically a percentage of what the bill is. Say you need X-rays and they're $1,000. If your coinsurance is 20% on you and your plan pays 80%, that means you'll owe $200.

COPAYMENT PLAN

Let's take the same X-ray example. If your copayment for X-rays is $150, it doesn't matter if the X-ray fee is $500, $1,000 or $10,000; you're paying $150 and your insurance pays the rest.

Unfortunately, there is no phenomenal way to tell which plan is better for you. Unless you have a crystal ball to look into the future and see which procedures you'll need over the next year, and then you call your doctor's office to see their rate for those procedures, it's a bit of a shot in the dark. If your doctor only charges $500 for an X-ray, the coinsurance person pays less than the copayment person, but if they charge $1,000, the copayment person pays less.

You'll likely be fine with either, so if it's a matter of choosing one plan over the other and if you don't anticipate having too many health procedures this year, go with whichever one has a lower monthly premium or covers your preferred doctors.

AFFORDABLE CARE ACT

In 2010, the Obama administration signed into law the Affordable Care Act, ACA (Obamacare), which includes a few important provisions. First, if you're under twenty-six, you can stay on your parent's health insurance. This helps you bridge the gap between school and finding a job while remaining covered. Also, you can start with part-time or freelance jobs to build a resume without having to worry about benefits. Another important provision is that you cannot be denied coverage due to pre-existing conditions. Healthcare. gov has a lot of great ACA information in an easy, digestible format.

LIFE INSURANCE

This will be cheaper if you get it when you're younger. For every new age bracket you enter, for every new wrinkle that appears on your forehead, the premium goes up. There's no magic age for getting life insurance— it's whatever feels best for you. I've been offered life insurance through companies I've worked for and have always taken it. I've also had it independently when work didn't offer it. It's roughly $10/month or less and will help my family plan a kick-ass funeral party for me if anything were to happen.

When it comes to life insurance, do what feels right for your family to plan a proper funeral (or one hell of a party in your honor), to package up your items and store them for a while, and to even assist with grief counseling or therapy in your absence. If you have kids, it might be nice to get covered so they're taken care of should anything happen. No one likes to think about these things, but it's important to make sure loved ones are cared for.

SHORT TERM DISABILITY

A lot of companies are now offering this through supplementary or secondary insurance companies (think Aflac). If you have a family history of people getting sick young, if you are someone whose company doesn't offer much in terms of sick leave or benefits, if you plan to start a family soon, or if you have a mental health issue and predict you may require some time off, look into some options. These typically aren't expensive, but if you don't see the need for this type of insurance, you could consider skipping it.

For all types of insurance, the best advice is to be realistic. As much as I would love to live a millennium like Methuselah (and still retire at sixty, of course), that just isn't realistic. At some point, I'll get sick. At some point, I'll die. I can't change facts.

SHIT ADULTS NEVER TAUGHT US

All we can do right now is assume the best but plan for the worst. Know yourself and what you can afford but also think through what you would do in a worst-case scenario and plan as much as your budget allows.

Regardless, it's important to be covered, so always have insurance. You never know what could happen.

NEGOTIATE WITH DOCTORS

This concept will likely freak out some of you. To be very clear, do not negotiate your health. Of course, your health comes first. I mean that you should negotiate the *bill*.

Did you even know you could do that? I didn't for a long time.

Let's start with a bit of terminology before we walk through the steps. There's something called "reasonable and customary" that insurance companies use to negotiate down your bill before they pay their part. Let's pretend you got an X-ray and the doctor's office charged the insurance company $1,500. The insurance company looks at similar doctors' offices in your area who are doing similar X-ray procedures and says, "Whoa. Are you insane, Doc? Almost everyone else is doing these services for like $600. That's what we'll pay. $600."

Then the insurance company pays their part, and you pay yours. You'll often see two columns on the "explanation of benefits" (that paper they send you before the bill that you probably throw away because it says "this is not a bill"). One column will usually say "Amount billed"; the other will say something fancy like "Member rate" or "Amount allowed." That's because your insurance company hires people to negotiate on your behalf, so they pay the doctor less and so do you.

Do you want to know something awesome? You can do the same thing. Especially if you don't have insurance.

It's always easier to do this before a procedure but it's definitely possible after, too, once you've already received the bill.

First, you'll usually have to call your doctor's office and ask to speak with the billing department. Set aside half an hour to do this. These things take time, especially if you're calling a hospital's billing department. Those guys are busy.

Before you call, check the reasonable and customary rates for that procedure and be prepared to use those rates as leverage. Remember Kelly Bluebook? They're the people who tell you a good price for a car. The same thing exists for healthcare. It's called Healthcare Bluebook. Use their "free tool" and type in the kind of procedure you've received and your zip code. The website will generate a range of rates related to that procedure (lowest, low, normal, and high). There are similar companies to Healthcare Bluebook, too. Just search online for "healthcare fair price estimate" and a few should pop up. Most are free.

Next, when you speak with the doctor's office, ask for a copy of the bill if you don't have one yet. You can request an itemized bill, just like I mentioned for the car, to see if there are any hidden fees. Sometimes even just asking for it drops the rate even lower. They don't want you to know they are charging you $35 for a pair of latex surgical gloves.

Be nice and pull at some heartstrings. When you call the doctor's office, always be polite. It's a negotiation and yelling will get you nowhere. Just explain that you can't afford the bill right now, you didn't expect this large of a payment, and you'd like to work with them on it. You can say you've done research and while you understand they charge $1,500 for this type of procedure, based on what you've seen, the standard is less than half that.

Once you've agreed upon a rate, feel free to ask about a payment plan so you can pay in installments. Just know that sometimes they'll go even lower if you offer to pay it all at once.

If you're not getting anywhere with the doctor's office, there are third parties who can sometimes help. Not all doctor's offices or hospitals have a billing department; sometimes they send you to a "patient advocate," and that person will talk you through your payment options.

Sometimes they'll pull things like, "Well, this is what the lab we use charges," to which you can say, "I chose the doctor, not the lab." Sometimes they'll say things like, "We have a fixed rate for our services," to which you can say, "Is it the same fixed rate offered under reasonable and customary practices with your partnering insurance companies? If I call a major insurer, will they tell me they pay the same rate?" But you know—nicely.

One last thought: there is a chance your insurance company never even paid. I had a doctor's appointment in August of 2020 and then in December received a bill for $800 in lab work. I emailed my doctor's office and said, "I just received the attached bill from the lab. It looks very high considering I'm insured. Can your billing department please take a look this week and see if anything looks off on your end before I call the lab next week?" The doctor's office called me later that day and said, "I spoke with the lab and they said they submitted the bill to your insurance but they never responded. They're calling your insurance company again this week but don't pay anything yet." If I had just paid the bill, I would have wound up paying a way higher amount just because my insurance company was feeling lazy.

Don't give up. Some doctors are like car salesmen in lab coats. They want to be paid as much as possible. You can win this.

Give It A Fucking Shot

☐ Get an itemized copy of your bill by contacting the doctor's office.

☐ Look up the procedure online for a fair price range.

☐ Call your doctor's accounting department.

☐ Negotiate your bill down kindly but firmly.

☐ Either pay all at once (which tends to be cheaper) or set up a payment plan directly with the doctor's office.

NEGOTIATE YOUR MONTHLY BILLS

You know how when you sign up for your Internet, cable, or mobile provider, they always seem to have an introductory price? They're so proud of it. They send you constant emails and postcards boasting about how very special they are because of this very special rate and how very special you'd be if you signed up. You swoon, because of course you do. Who doesn't want to feel special?

And a year later, when the honeymoon phase has worn off and you're no longer the apple of their eye, your rate jumps. No warning, no kind email saying, "Hey, we're about to fuck you over and not tell you. Hope that's cool."

There are a few ways to get your lovely introductory rate back. Search online for what the provider is offering new customers and bookmark it. Now go to their competitor(s) website and see what they're offering. Bookmark that, too.

Next, call your provider. Ask for the sales department but don't get comfortable there. Tell the salesperson what's going on. Tell them that you had a beautiful, low rate and that it has gone up. What they'll typically do is explain to you that that rate was only good for a year and now you are receiving their "regular customer rate," or however they phrase it. Let them tell you that, and then ask for their cancelation department.

One of two things is going to happen there. Either:

1. The salesperson will ask you if there is

anything they can do, to which you say, "Yes. I want my amazing rate back. Can you do that?" If they say no, continue to #2. If they say "Yes," stupendous. You're done.

2. They will transfer you to the cancelation department.

You'll likely end up in the cancelation department. That's okay. You want this to happen. They have more power than the sales department.

The sales department has a handful of offers they're allowed to extend. Almost none of them apply to current customers. In sales, their main purpose is to bring in new people. You're old news.

The cancelation department (or "customer retention department" or "purgatory of customer service representatives department") has more power than the sales department in keeping current customers.

Simply tell them that you want to cancel your account. They'll ask why you'd do such a harsh thing to them. I mean, you were just getting to know each other. You tell them you have a better offer and since their sales department won't match it, you're taking the other provider's offer.

No one likes being dumped for a younger, hotter model.

They'll try to convince you to stay. Now, here's the key: you have to be good with walking away. You also have to be good at leaving out some information.

Maybe your company, Company A, enrolled you at $50/month for the first year and now they've jacked you up to $80/month. Company B offers you $45/month, but they also have a $99/setup fee. When you're negotiating with Company A, ignore the setup fee completely. Pretend it doesn't exist; like a red flag in the first few months of a new relationship, you look right past it.

If Company A says they'll give you your previous rate back, great. Even if you saw that Company A now offers new customers $40/month, it's okay to settle for what you had. Let's be honest, you weren't even going to know about the $40/month if they hadn't put you through all of this.

Sometimes negotiations land somewhere in the middle of your old lower rate and your jacked-up new one. My Internet company billed me $50/month for 100 mbps broadband speed. After a year, my rate went up to $70/month, so I called them. They were unable to get me back down to $50/month with my current plan but said they could offer me $55/month for 300 mbps broadband speed. I am tripling my speed and they're getting an extra $5/month out of me for basically doing no work. Cool, that felt like a win-win.

Here's the sad part. If they won't come down to a number you're comfortable with, you'll have to breakup. Cancel your existing service and switch to the competitor. People do it all the time. I myself have bounced back and forth between the two Internet providers offered in my area in order to get a lower rate.

You probably won't have to do that, though. These companies don't want to send out a tech to reinstall your Internet in a year. They don't want to lose a customer, either, and for some representatives, their commission depends on keeping people.

Some companies offer this entire process I just described through online chat. You're more than welcome to do it that way, just know that you probably won't get as good of a rate. The chat is often automated or assigned to a sales representative outside of the country, so they're set to a script. If you're able to call, I highly recommend it.

You may have to do this every year as your Internet provider attempts to raise your rate. Just keep an eye on your bill and get ready to go through the process every so often. They know it's coming. Let them work to keep you.

This process isn't exclusive to Internet companies. You can apply this process to mobile phone, home phone, cable TV, or any other subscription services. If your rate has changed, or if you've seen a different rate advertised elsewhere, call to negotiate it.

Give It A Fucking Shot

- ☐ Download copies of your bill from both before and after the price increase.

- ☐ Research competing companies to get introductory rates. Keep those handy.

- ☐ Call the company and start in the sales department. Ask them to lower your rate back down.

- ☐ If they refuse, have them transfer you to the cancelation department and ask them to lower your rate back down.

- ☐ If nothing works, switch companies. You already know the rates they offer—just call and set up a new account.

KNOW ABOUT TAX WITHHOLDINGS AND DEDUCTIONS

A new job comes with a lot of paperwork. You'll get a W-4, an I-9, and what feels like a million other pieces of paper.

If you're an independent contractor, you'll get a 1099—which means no taxes are taken out from your paycheck but you'll owe a large lump sum at the end of the year. Most jobs, however, are filed with a W-4, which is where taxes are taken out of each paycheck so when you file taxes at the end of the year, you owe less and potentially even get a refund.

A section that a lot of people stumble on when completing a W-4 form is tax-withholding elections (or personal allowances). For some reason no one ever talked to us about this when we were kids. I guess it's not an ideal topic for Saturday morning cartoons.

Basically, this is the amount of money you've agreed to pay the government as part of their grand guessing game called "income tax."

If you elect "0", you're saying to the government, "Take my money now but when refund time comes around, you better owe me, punk." You're having a larger amount of money taken out of your usual paycheck but will likely get a bigger refund at the end of the year.

If you elect "1", you're claiming yourself as a dependent and saying to the government, "I'm a strong independent person who needs my money now and we can settle this later." You'll get a bigger paycheck up front than a zero election, but it may mean a smaller refund or even that you owe money come April 15th (Tax Day). It's a closer "guess" of what the government will want from you than claiming zero dependents.

If you elect "2" or more, you're claiming more people (most likely family) as dependents, and saying to the government, "I've got people to take care of so give me more money, get off my back and I'll pay you back later." You'll get more in your paycheck, but taxes may get more complicated and you'll likely end up owing more when taxes are due.

There are a lot of paycheck calculators online (like PaycheckCity) to help you figure out which option is right for you. When you get a new job, you can input the salary, state, paycheck frequency, and any other benefits to calculate various withholdings to see what you're comfortable with.

Now that you're all set up with your fancy new paycheck, let's talk about tax deductions. This is relevant when tax season rolls around, which, despite my complaining, seems to happen every year.

If you make $100,000 a year and owe $24,000 (24%) in federal taxes, roughly $24,000 will be taken from your paycheck over the course of the year. Let's say you elected "1" as your withholding and you ended up paying a total of $23,000 through your paychecks that year so the government says, "You owe me $1,000, pay up." What you can do is deduct expenses you've had that were work-related to bring that amount down. Say you had to purchase a computer so you could work from home. That computer cost $2,000. That doesn't mean you deduct $2,000 from the $1,000 you owe. That means you deduct $2,000 from the $100,000 you make and now you are paying 24% of $98,000 (which is $23,520, so you only owe $520 to the government, instead of $1,000).

The government offers "standard deductions," which is a rate they've decided everyone can deduct. In 2020, standard deductions were $12,400, so if you didn't spend more than $12,400 on business expenses, you can just take that deduction and call it a day. Now you're paying taxes on $87,600 instead of $100,000. If you did spend more than $12,400, then you itemize those expenses and get a bigger tax cut.

Deductions can include any cost you've incurred for your job, like buying a new computer, a uniform for work, or the cost of training courses or classes. You can also deduct things that weren't directly related to work, like charitable donations, mortgage or student loan interest, or a portion of childcare. If you're self-employed, you can often claim more items, including mileage.

Make sense? No? Get a tax consultant to help you navigate. It's money well spent. Or skip to the next section and let free tax software guide you through the process.

Give It A Fucking Shot

☐ Find an online calculator and figure out which withholding amount is right for you. Then adjust your withholding amount with your company.

☐ When it comes time for taxes, make a list of everything you could deduct and see if it's more or less than standard deductions.

☐ If you're still confused, find a tax consultant or use tax software to guide you through deductions.

DO YOUR TAXES

I'm going to start this chapter by saying that I have no idea how to do my taxes. You know who does know? The Internet. There are huge companies that make it their sole purpose to help you do your taxes. They also want to make money doing it, so here are some things you need to know to avoid paying them more than they deserve.

I'm just going to say it. Doing your taxes sucks. It sucks more if you're doing them last minute while scrambling to find the stuff you need to do them properly.

Taxes are due in April. April 15th, actually. That doesn't mean you should start doing taxes the night before they are due. This isn't college. Gather your various tax documents, list of deductions, bank letters, proof of insurance, and any other documents you may need ahead of time.

Want to know something not fun? The government knows how much you owe or how much they should pay you, but they've decided it's a more fun not to tell you. It's like a word problem in math class except if you refuse to participate, you don't get sent to time out, you get fined and sent to jail. Approach taxes like a group project instead of a homework assignment and get some assistance.

In this case, your assistance will come from the Internet. There are a few different types of software, online ones specifically, that offer tax services for free or minimal cost, but be careful. These types of software build in a lot of traps to try to get you to pay more than you need to.

FIND A JOB

Wow. Such a daunting task, right? Find a job. Sure, let me just run out to the store and pick one of those up.

We say "find a job" like it's effortless. You spend your childhood being asked what you want to be when you grow up as if whenever you get there you can just be that. But the fact of the matter is that no one's going to hand you a job because in fourth grade you told your class that you wanted it.

Luckily, we live in a time where the Internet exists. We aren't printing out hundreds of resumes, going to the post office, spending tons of money on stamps to mail them out, and then waiting for weeks to hear back.

Today's application process is much faster and much cheaper—as in, free.

So why do some people remain jobless? Well, the short answer is there are a million reasons: systemic problems, the high cost of higher education, a struggling economy. Like we talked about in earlier sections, Millennials (and Gen Z-ers) entered the job market during and after the 2008 recession, so they've had to climb a corporate staircase that started four stories below ground.

Those topics are far too deeply rooted to address in this particular chapter. But there is one main reason people remain jobless that we *can* address: most people get stuck on the idea of what they *should* be doing instead of the idea of what they *could* be doing.

People use excuses like, "Well I've only ever done this job so I can't switch fields now," or, "I don't know how to use this software, so I can't get a job that uses it." Of course you can. If you've learned how to do everything that got you to this point, you can learn a new software. Since "find a job" is such a big task, let's divide it into smaller tasks.

MAKE LISTS

Not a list of jobs you want. I don't care what jobs you think you want right now. You're instead going to make two lists.

First List:
I want you to write a list of qualities you want in a job. Do you want to work at a big company or a small company? Do you want to work autonomously, or as part of a team? Do you want to work at a computer, or would you rather be more active? Would you prefer more analytical work, or would you prefer to work with your hands? Do you want work at a place where you can grow, or do you want to work somewhere that will help build you up and prepare you for the next thing? Do you want to travel for work, or stay in one place?

Second List:
I want you to write a list of qualities you want to bring to a job. Do you want to be creative? Do you want to write? Do you want to build or make a product? Do you want to help others?

Next, take these lists and grab keywords from them like "creative," "team," and "build." Start by entering those words into a job board website (like Indeed, LinkedIn, or ZipRecruiter). If you have a specific job title in mind, places like LinkedIn let you search for a specific job title, location, and then keywords.

Not everyone uses the same terminology for job postings. You may think you want a "Project Manager" role so you search only those, but then someone posts the perfect "Production Supervisor" role that's exactly what you're looking for. They're just calling it something different.

You may think you want to work in music but by searching keywords instead of certain companies or job titles, you find a music position at an advertising agency that's way more within reach.

APPLY EVERY DAY

Remember how I said that before the Internet people had to print out resumes and then go to the post office and mail them? Well, you don't. You just have to get on a computer or phone. So apply every day. If you need to find a job quickly, apply to twenty or thirty a day. If you have a job but are looking to make a move soon, apply to one a day.

Just don't lose momentum. Make it part of your morning routine. Make coffee, check Instagram, and then head to your favorite job listings website and apply to five jobs.

PUT RESUMES IN YOUR CAR OR BAG

I know I just said you don't need to print resumes, but I lied. You don't need them to apply but you should have them on hand for interviews. If you're applying a lot, chances are someone's going to reach out to you and say, "Hey, we love your experience. Can you come in this afternoon to meet?" Go. Take the meeting. Just be sure to bring a resume with you. If you have a stack in your car, you'll never have to worry about forgetting one.

BROADEN YOUR SEARCH

This could mean a lot of things. It could mean expanding the range in which you're willing to commute, looking for remote work instead of in-person only, and alternating keywords when you search, such as manager, supervisor, department head, or lead. Whatever that looks like to you, just try it.

PRACTICE INTERVIEW

If you've gone on a few interviews and aren't hearing back, practice some interviews with friends. Have them ask you questions you aren't prepared for. Go online and research the twenty most common interview questions and practice those. Reference the skills noted in the *Negotiate Your Salary* and *Negotiate Your Raise* chapters of this book.

FOLLOW UP

After you've interviewed somewhere and you really want the job, send the recruiter a quick thank you. It should be simple and short. Write something like, "Thank you for your time today. It was wonderful meeting you, and I hope to hear from you soon." If they mentioned something specific in the interview, you can follow up on that. Maybe they asked you your start date and you weren't sure at that moment. In that case, you could say, "It was great meeting you today. I've checked the calendar and would be available to start two weeks from Monday. Please let me know if you have any other questions I can answer."

DON'T GET DISCOURAGED

Nothing kills a job prospect like the loss of confidence. If you give off the vibe that you're desperate or that you need the job, you probably won't get it. It's like a first date. No one wants to date the needy person, and no one wants to hire the desperate person. Show your confidence to prove the level of self-assurance you'll bring when you get the job. It can be hard but find things that make you feel confident. What makes you feel like a badass? Is it a certain outfit you like? Or calling a friend for a confidence boost before you walk in the door?

Just remember, you've got this. You'll do great. Now go get the fucking job.

DON'T DATE PEOPLE AT WORK

You know that awkward feeling when you have a fight with a classmate in October and then have to sit next to them for another six months in class? That's what it's like if you date someone at work.

You may find your soul mate and live happily ever after. Surely, you've heard the stories of people who have. But those people are the exception, not the rule. The rule is that you'll likely meet someone and have a great few weeks. Then you'll realize you see too much of each other because you're spending all day at work with them and then all your free time with them. Your coworkers might start to distance themselves from you because they don't want to be dragged into your relationship. Eventually you discover there's a text chain about you and your new beau that you're not on.

Of course, if you break up, that's a whole other story. You'll have to deal with the awkwardness of working every day with a person who now represents a painful memory. How can you move on when you're seeing them all the time? What happens when they start dating someone else and your workday is now filled with jealousy? God forbid they start dating someone else at work—talk about awkward.

Plus, now you've possibly lost your work BFF. Who are you going to talk to about John's loud breathing or Linda's constant pen clicking? Your relationship will likely transition from awkward to unbearable. Inevitably, one or both of you will leave a company you likely wouldn't have left otherwise.

Recognize that most of the time your feelings about someone

you work with are purely a work crush. You're into this person because you spend over forty hours a week next to them. If you spend that much time with anyone, you'll start to have a crush on them. It's basically socially acceptable Stockholm syndrome. I've had a crush on someone at every job I've ever had. Once I leave the job, those crushes fade after a few weeks and I realize I mostly liked the person because they were nearby, and I was bored at work. My mind was wandering, or I was attracted to their confidence or work persona. That's not who they really are, though. Or rather, that's not the full picture.

If you leave a job, a few weeks pass, and your crush is still intact, then by all means reach out. It's way less problematic now and who knows, maybe it was meant to be, but you no longer have the pressure of staying together to avoid making your work life uncomfortable.

If you're truly set on dating someone at work, try to make it someone who isn't in your department. Date someone who's temporary and won't be around long. Date someone who can transfer to a different office or division if things go south.

There are over seven billion people on the planet. Don't make your future self suffer because you had to date the one tolerable person who was closest to you most weekdays.

LOVE YOUR COWORKERS

Ew. Not in a gross way. In a completely normal way. Didn't you read the *Don't Date People at Work* chapter?

I've always said that "loving work" is split into two parts. Half is loving the work you do, and the other half is loving the people you do it with (again, get your mind out of the gutter). You could have the greatest job in the world at the most amazing company with all the prestige you desired, but if you're miserable because your coworkers are mean assholes, you'll dread going in every day.

Ideally you would know whether you like the people you'll be working with before you take the job, but that's not usually possible. Your best option is to check online for a sense of workplace culture, with sites like Glassdoor being wonderfully helpful.

You're never going to love everyone you work with. Chances are, you'll have bad days here and there. The goal is to have a balance of more good days than bad. Even if you wouldn't hang out with these people outside of work, you appreciate that you get to work alongside them during the time you are together.

All new jobs take time to get used to. You're the new kid, so everyone might not be super friendly and warm at the beginning. Don't take it personally, but don't let it slide too long. It's normal if it's a busy time where everyone is hyper focused and can't take time to become your new work BFF. But if a few months go by and things have calmed down yet you're still getting the cold shoulder, it might be time to start reassessing where you are.

It's normal to get attached to one person, too. There's almost always someone who you could see yourself being friends with outside of work. These are your work BFFs, or even your "Work Wives" or "Work Husbands." They probably keep you sane during the day and listen to you vent when a client or another coworker did something shitty. Be careful not to form a clique, though. No one likes the office mean girls.

So what do you do if you've been at your job for six months, no one even acknowledges you when you walk in in the morning, and you leave work each day miserable because of the interactions you've had? You leave.

Chances are, the job you have is similar to positions at other companies. You want to love your job—it's where you spend a lot of your time—but if people are making you miserable, that's as valid a reason as any to move on. Begin your job hunt before you officially quit and when you've found the right replacement, go for it.

KNOW WHEN IT'S TIME TO LEAVE A JOB

I've always had two rules for knowing when it's time to leave a job.

The first is when I start dreading Sunday nights. Like, seriously dreading. Not the standard, "Oh shit the weekend is over, it flew by so fast" type of dread. I mean the debilitating, anxiety-ridden, depressing kind of dread. If you're trying to bend time to stop Monday morning from happening, it's time to find a new job.

Life's too short to dread five days a week to only enjoy the remaining two.

The second rule is when I know I've gotten everything out of the job that I possibly could. When it begins to feel like I'm living the same day over and over again. That's fine for a while but eventually, I've stopped learning. If I'm not growing and there's nowhere for me to move up to within the company, then I know it's time to leave.

If you want to leave for the second reason and you like where you're working, ask if there is another office or another department you can transfer to. Maybe a promotion is possible if you stick it out another six months, but you'd only know by asking the executives.

If there's nowhere to go within the company and you'll be stuck in this role for the foreseeable future, then it's time to begin looking elsewhere.

Since you've already got a job, you're in an excellent position to find a new one. You're not going to settle because you desperately need money. You're going to be specific about what you want because you can pinpoint the parts of your current position you wish were different.

Start by going through the steps in the *Find A Job* chapter. Make a list of the qualities you want in the next company you work for, as well as the skills you'd like to utilize. Then slowly start to apply. The last time I began looking for new jobs, I applied to one every morning before I headed out the door to work. It became part of my routine. Sometimes I would apply to one more before bed, especially if I had had a revelation that day about the type of job I wanted, or realized something about my current job that I didn't want to carry over to the next one.

Take your time and make your move wisely. Once you leave, you can't turn back easily, so be as sure as you can that the move you make is the right one.

I love a good pros and cons list. If you can, compare each new offer you get to your current job and see if there are any glaring holes in what you really want to be doing.

If it doesn't work out, you can always move again, but it'll be hard to move back. Be sure that what you're stepping into is a better fit than your current position.

Give It A Fucking Shot

- ☐ Sign up for one or two job-listing websites such as LinkedIn, ZipRecruiter, or Indeed.

- ☐ Make a profile, upload your resume, and update your contact information.

- ☐ Apply to jobs every day. Even if it's just one.

- ☐ Print resume copies to keep in your car or bag.

- ☐ Send a follow-up after an interview thanking them for their time.

- ☐ Keep your chin up. You're doing great and will get a job in no time.

"YOU WILL NEVER ALWAYS BE MOTIVATED, SO YOU MUST LEARN TO BE DISCIPLINED."

— UNKNOWN

EXPAND YOUR JOB DESCRIPTION

I once led a team of about ten people. One day, nine of them were super busy—I'm talking totally slammed. They were running around, doing crazy stuff to get their jobs done. One guy wasn't busy at all because his department didn't have much to do that day. I asked him if he could help out, so his coworkers don't drop on the floor from exhaustion and his response to me was, "That's not really part of my job."

Do you think the other nine people were doing only the things that were in their job description? Hell no. Half of them offered to jump in and help when they saw the others struggling.

When the time came for us to evaluate employees and discuss raises, guess who didn't get my vote for a raise? Yup, Mister "That's Not in My Job Description."

I love people who expand their job description. That shows that they're part of the team, rather than an island by themselves. I knew they'd be a good fit when people came in to interview and said, "I also know how to..." or, "I'm not sure of the entirety of what this position entails, but in my role now I also handle...."

For example, I hired a receptionist one time because she actually asked in the interview if she could help out with social media marketing. We were looking for someone to help with that, but it wasn't in the job posting. She took it upon herself during the interview to mention, "I noticed you have a Facebook and Instagram but there don't seem to be many posts. Would that be something I could help take on in this role?"

I loved it. Of course, we'd love for you to help us with other stuff. Hired!

After a few months of being at any job, once you've finally gotten down the basics of your role without breaking into a cold sweat, you usually start to get a little bored.

That's a good time to see if there is anything else that feels adjacent to your role. You've been at the company for a while, so you've likely seen some gaps in the workflow. You now have enough of a handle on your role to contribute in a different way.

I worked at a company where we ordered lunch to be delivered every day. I noticed that day after day the receptionist struggled to pick a place. Ultimately, we ended up eating at the same nine or ten spots, despite living in a city with some of the best restaurants in the country.

In my downtime, I made a spreadsheet that consisted of over sixty nearby restaurants. It listed whether or not they deliver, their distance from the office, the type of cuisine they served, their hours, and then a date column so we could write in the last time we ordered from them.

The receptionist was ecstatic. When a client asked for a specific type of cuisine, she didn't have to look up nearby places because we already had a few to choose from on the list.

I did the same thing a few months later when I noticed that new clients were having a hard time locating our office. We were in a big complex and the route to get to our building was a bit confusing. One day, I made a one-sheet PDF that showed a map of the complex, a star marking where we were located, an outline of where clients could park, and our phone number. This could be easily attached to any email to new clients so that we didn't have to explain how to find us to each person.

I bet there's a way that you can help fill in some of the gaps at your workplace. Try to notice this week if there is something you or a coworker is stumbling with that could have a fairly easy solution. If it's something that will take an hour to help solve but save countless headaches in the future, go for it.

For example, TurboTax's regular account lets you file for free if you're the most basic bitch in the world. You only had one job, you're taking standard deductions, you didn't donate to charity or have student loans. You get the point. Super basic level is free. Everything else costs money even though it's advertised as free.

H&R Block is very similar. So are other services like TaxSlayer, TaxAct, and Credit Karma. A simple search result for "Online Tax Services" will give you hundreds of options. If you want to take the time and see which ones are actually free or the lowest cost, it might be worth your trouble.

If scrolling through dozens of options isn't worth it to you, keep reading. I did the work for you.

Each of the major softwares have an *actually* free software. For TurboTax, it's called the "TurboTax Free File Program." For H&R Block, it's called the "H&R Block IRS Free File." The issue is, their standard softwares also make you think they're free. TurboTax's regular program is called TurboTax Free Edition but it's only free for certain people (those basic bitches mentioned above). The Free File Program covers way more options and a lot more people.

It's kind of like an all-inclusive resort. They all say everything is included but only some of them actually mean it. Free Editions are like an advertised breakfast buffet, but all you really get is a dry bagel, unless you want to pay extra for the "premium options." IRS Free File Editions are the actual breakfast buffet, complete with all the omelet toppings you want.

It's important to note that even the IRS Free File options are only available for certain people but the range of people who get free filing is way bigger than the standard websites. The threshold is usually people who make about $60,000 - $70,000 or less a year, but it changes year to year.

If you want to file for free, search for "IRS Free File" to see if you qualify and then to see which sites offer Free File services.

If you didn't do any crazy shit last year, like working fifteen jobs and owning two companies, doing your taxes should only take a couple of hours.

I know it sucks, but you can make it fun. Invite over a friend and do your taxes together. Play some music. Take a dance break every half hour or reward yourself with takeout when your taxes are done.

Okay. So you finally file your taxes, for free if possible, way before the deadline. You get your nice little refund check, cash it, buy a new laptop (which is likely deductible next year). All is awesome. Done and done.

Not quite. The IRS can audit you for up to six years, so keep your tax returns in an envelope somewhere in the back of a closet, next to your eighth-grade band uniform, for up to six years after you file them. Then you can start having yearly bonfires for the ones older than that.

I promise, you can do this. Here are some easy steps to follow.

Give It A Fucking Shot

☐ In February or March, pick a random week-night or Sunday afternoon to do your taxes and then stick to it.

☐ In the days leading up to your Tax Day, get a big envelope and gather all of your 1099s, your W-2s, and any bank statements or tax documents that come in the mail.

☐ Google "IRS Free File" and find software you're comfortable using.

☐ Sign up and set aside three to four hours to do your taxes. Do them with a friend or with some music playing—just do them.

☐ Then print out a copy and save them some-where for six years.

CREATE A SOLID RESUME

I have bad news for you—when an amazing job becomes available, that hiring manager gets hundreds if not thousands of resumes. Take less than an hour now and give yourself a better chance against those other bozos. Seriously, just go do it.

First up, the layout. Everyone does the same thing with their layout, because everyone took the same Microsoft Word class in fifth grade. You're better than that. Be creative. Just don't add pictures of yourself or a million fonts. Keep it simple.

You can even Google "Microsoft Word Resume Templates Free" and see if any of those strike your fancy.

Here's a quick checklist that will help you with the layout of your resume.

QUICK CHECKLIST FOR LAYOUT

☐ **NAME:** Centered at the top

☐ **CONTACT INFO:** Include your email, phone number, city, and state. Only include your full address if you're interested in a brand-new stalker.

☐ **MISSION STATEMENT:** These used to be cool but now they're weird. Your mission is to get the job you're applying for. They already know that. Only include it if it says something your prospective employer wouldn't know from your resume already. If you don't know what to say, leave it out.

☐ **EMPLOYMENT HISTORY:** The main event. Add your employment history towards the top, before the other sections.

☐ **EMPLOYMENT DESCRIPTION:** Include three or four bullet points under each employment item describing what your position entailed. Use active language instead of passive language. For example, instead of writing "Managed system integration," write, "Manage system integration." Active language makes you sound like you could do it again if you wanted to.

☐ **EDUCATION:** Where did you learn the stuff you know? High School? College? Clown School? Keep it to a maximum of three schools.

☐ **SKILLS AND SOFTWARE:** What are you good at? You can list skills and software in the same section or in different sections. Just make sure they're clearly distinguished as separate pieces.

☐ **OTHER STUFF:** If you need to fill in more space, try adding two or three hobbies so that your prospective employer gets to know you. Include any awards, certificates, and external training you can boast about.

Stuck on what to include?

Let's start with some software ideas to get the noodle cooking. You can include cloud-based software (Google Drive, Dropbox), word processors (Microsoft Word or Excel), software from your last job (Salesforce, Trello, Slack, QuickBooks), software you learned in school (Adobe, Keynote, WordPress), and software you use in your day-to-day life (Zoom, VSCO). Skills to list on your resume include "detail oriented," "deadline driven," "highly organized," your typing speed, and your personality strengths. The skills should be relevant to the type of job you're applying for and specific to you. If you're applying to be a stunt driver, your skills should reflect your reaction time, precision handling, and *safety precautions*. If you're applying to be a nanny, your skills should reflect your patience, your creativity, and your *safety precautions*. There's going to be overlap for many positions, but obviously the safety precautions for a stunt driver are (hopefully) very different than those of a nanny, so be specific when you can.

In bullets under each position you've held, include information about daily projects, weekly assignments, or even one-off tasks you may have assisted with. How were you involved with clients? How were you involved with your team? Did you help with other departments? Did you help switch software? Did you manage any projects? Did you build client lists? Did you assist with sales or marketing?

This is your moment to gloat. Write down everything you've done that was spectacular. You're handing someone a single page introduction of you, so show how incredible you are. There's no need to be humble in this section.

With regard to your position descriptions, use a variety of language. Don't start every employment bullet point with "manage" when you could instead use "oversee," "supervise," "lead," "spearhead," "administer," "guide," "liaise," "maintain," "usher," or "handle." There are enough synonyms to avoid repeating yourself too often.

Your resume should be one page. I promise you—everything fits on one page. If it doesn't, format it differently. Drop off the old stuff. Remove the software you don't actually know that well. Take off hobbies. Split things into columns. It's always possible to get it on one page.

Here's a quick template to use as a jumping-off point.

NAME

PHONE NUMBER | CITY / STATE / ZIP CODE | EMAIL

EMPLOYMENT

DATE (ex: 4/2017- 7/2020)
LOCATION (ex: LOS ANGELES, CA)

POSITION TITLE | COMPANY
- STUFF I DID
- STUFF I DID
- STUFF I DID
- STUFF I DID

DATE
LOCATION

POSITION TITLE | COMPANY
- STUFF I DID
- STUFF I DID
- STUFF I DID
- STUFF I DID

DATE
LOCATION

POSITION TITLE | COMPANY
- STUFF I DID
- STUFF I DID
- STUFF I DID
- STUFF I DID

SOFTWARE

- STUFF I KNOW HOW TO USE
- STUFF I KNOW HOW TO USE
- STUFF I KNOW HOW TO USE
- STUFF I KNOW HOW TO USE

- STUFF I KNOW HOW TO USE
- STUFF I KNOW HOW TO USE
- STUFF I KNOW HOW TO USE
- STUFF I KNOW HOW TO USE

- STUFF I KNOW HOW TO USE
- STUFF I KNOW HOW TO USE
- STUFF I KNOW HOW TO USE
- STUFF I KNOW HOW TO USE

SKILLS

- STUFF I'M GOOD AT
- STUFF I'M GOOD AT
- STUFF I'M GOOD AT

- STUFF I'M GOOD AT
- STUFF I'M GOOD AT
- STUFF I'M GOOD AT

- STUFF I'M GOOD AT
- STUFF I'M GOOD AT
- STUFF I'M GOOD AT

EDUCATION

GRADUATION DATE
LOCATION

SCHOOL NAME
DEGREE

GRADUATION DATE
LOCATION

SCHOOL NAME
DEGREE

GRADUATION DATE
LOCATION

SCHOOL NAME
DEGREE

So, what if you're not job searching right now? You want to know the worst time to compile a resume? When you are job searching. There is no way you're going to remember everything you did in your current position when you're also stressed about money and what you're going to do with your life.

I recommend that you brush up your resume at least once a year. Here are a few questions to ask yourself when updating it.

- Did I learn anything new this year (like software), including outside of work?
- Did I take on any additional roles at my current company that are worth including?
- Did I help any teams outside of my usual projects?

You never know when you might be job hunting. You never know when a friend might reach out with the perfect opportunity if you send a resume right this second. Why not have one ready to go for that moment?

ACCEPT THAT DREAMS
TAKE WORK

When I first moved to Los Angeles, I met an endless stream of people who had moved there to be actors, directors, writers, artists, or musicians. After a while, it became apparent that some of those people thought moving to a city where art is made would be enough. That somehow, just by being there, amazing opportunities would fall in their lap. They hadn't looked around to see that there are a million people just like them wanting the same dream but working way harder to achieve it.

Let's take actors, for example. I have friends who moved to Los Angeles, got a part-time job to pay the bills, took some headshot photos, and even got an agent. Once they'd done all of that, they stopped putting in the effort. Then they would complain that they'd been there for two years and nothing was happening. They weren't taking classes, networking, finding work on their own, or creating work with friends. If they did get an audition, they'd be rusty because they hadn't practiced acting in a while and then the auditions wouldn't go well.

Then come the excuses.

> "I can't get new headshots. I need a haircut, I need to lose weight, I'm saving up for the best photographer."

> "I can't get work. My manager doesn't send me out. My reel isn't strong enough."

So many excuses.

If you need a haircut, get one. If you need a stronger reel, film some stuff on an iPhone with friends and make one. The same is true for just about every field. No one's going to hand you your dream. Even once you get it, you have to keep working for it. You think every famous writer wrote one book and then was like, "Awesome, now they'll just give me Pulitzers."? Nope. Steven Spielberg isn't just waiting around for awards; he's working his ass off on each job to deserve them.

Dreams take work. Because of course they do. You're turning a fantasy into reality. You can't just think really hard about a unicorn and have it materialize in front of you. Trust me, my five-year-old self tried. It doesn't work.

Nothing is going to be given to you. The word "dreams" is deceiving because it sounds like you just close your eyes and they happen to you. They don't. You have to work at them, and it takes a lot of effort to get where you want to go. Chasing a dream can feel as trying as sitting next to an infant on a cross-country flight. But when you get there, when your dreams do come true, it'll be worth the work you put in.

I got really great advice from a teacher once about making dreams happen. "Since they always say, an overnight success really takes ten years, speed it up. Do one thing every day for your career." If you're an actor, do something each day, whether it's taking photos, submitting to a casting call, attending a networking event, a class, or a workshop, or practicing a scene with friends. If you're a writer, write something every day, even if it's half of a page and that half of a page isn't very good. If you're an athlete, practice every single day, go to tryouts, tape yourself and watch for areas to improve, and meet with scouts. If you're a musician, teach yourself a new song each week and practice it daily, write new music, and record and upload songs online.

If you're someone who needs structure beyond "do something every day," then create the structure. Set aside thirty minutes a day. Enter it into your calendar. Set a reminder. Just make the time. Nothing incredible ever happens if we just sit around and wait for it.

So get up. Believe in your badass self. And get to work.

BEAT OTHERS TO YOUR DREAM HOME

Ever find the perfect apartment or house for rent on Zillow, then go see it, only to confirm it's the drop-dead perfect place? You're already imagining where your coffee table and bookcases are going to go. You agree to jump through all of the hoops to get it: fill out an application, give them $25 for a credit check, and hope that all goes through so you can put down a security deposit.

Then you sit and wait, hoping you get it. Until you finally get the call...you didn't. Someone beat you to it.

How? Did they get their application in faster? Did they have better credit? Did they bribe the landlord with cupcakes?

There could be a ton of reasons why someone else got the place instead of you, but there are definitely a few things you can do to make sure it doesn't happen again.

CREDIT REPORT
When you begin looking for a new home, a day or two before you go to the open house, get a credit report for yourself and print out a bunch of copies.

You get one free credit report a year from each of the three major credit bureaus. Just run a report through one of them and print out copies of it.

You want it to be recent, so make sure you run it within a month or so of going to see places. Don't bring a credit report that's four months old since no one wants that.

SECURITY DEPOSIT

Bring a blank check with you when you go to look at places. Landlords want nothing more than to fill a vacancy quickly. If you walk in and are the perfect tenant, why not sign on the dotted line that day?

APPLICATION

Most places have a very standard application for renting. You can find blank standard applications online. Fill out the application and bring a bunch of copies with you. Also bring a pen with you just in case the landlord has their heart set on you doing *their* application.

GO SEE THE PLACE

Great! Now that you've done all the prep, go see some places. When you find your dream home, seek out the person leasing it and say, "Hi, I love this place. Here's a copy of my recent credit report that was generated within the past week and here's a copy of a standard application, although I am happy to fill out yours as well. I am motivated to rent and if possible, I'm prepared to give you a check for the security deposit and sign the lease today." You might blindside them with how insanely prepared you are, but at least you'll be one step ahead of everyone else.

And bring cupcakes. It couldn't hurt.

Give It A Fucking Shot

Pretend you're going to see five houses this weekend. Pack the following:

☐ Six (five plus one for safety) copies of a recent credit report (within the past month).

☐ Six copies of a standard application you've already filled out.

☐ Two blank checks (one for safety in case you fill it out wrong).

☐ At least one pen for filling out applications and signing the lease.

GET YOUR SECURITY DEPOSIT BACK

Why does no one ever want to give you a security deposit back? Probably because they've already spent it and feel they can get away with keeping it. No such luck, bucko.

There are a few ways to get a security deposit back. These are the legal ones.

First, always take pictures of a place when you move in. Walk around and take pictures of the entire apartment. Make sure you get all the walls, countertops, windows, doorways, and floors, or at least a good portion of them. Like an influencer's photoshoot for the gram, there's no such thing as too many pics.

When the photos are ready, email them to yourself that day. You can even email your new bestie, the landlord, too. Make sure the email is saved somewhere for when you move out. It's important to email them so the date is saved, instead of printing or saving them somewhere. By emailing them the day you move in, you're saying, "This is how it looked when I got here. Don't pin the damage the dude before made on me." This way they won't be able to blame you for that giant hole in the wall when you move out because you're proving it was there on move-in day. Also, don't move into a place with a giant hole in the wall. I'd be worried about you.

If you're about to move out and are just now reading this, that's okay. We can still get that security deposit back for you even if you didn't take pictures.

What's more important is that on the day you move out, you go through the exact same process. This time grab a newspaper with

the date on it (first find a place that still sells newspapers). Take the newspaper, walk around, take tons of photos with the newspaper in it, and email them all to yourself. The newspaper is to prove the pictures came from the day you moved out. They can't say, "How do we know these are the photos from the day you moved out and not three months before?" You can't take a photo with a newspaper from the future in it. You're not Marty McFly. If construction or the landlord damages something after you move out, they can't blame it on you. The photos prove the status of everything on the exact day you left.

Also, there's something called "normal wear and tear." You shouldn't be charged for chipping paint or a small stain on the carpet, because that's considered "normal wear and tear." What did they think, you were going to sit completely still in that apartment for a year like a porcelain doll?

Maybe you're a bit further down the road with the security deposit battle. You've already moved out and moved on, yet your old landlord won't give you your money back. Like an ex who won't return your favorite sweatshirt, they're being stubborn and childish. You know you left the place in pristine condition but they're being unfair. Ask for an itemized list of what they think you "broke" along with the associated monetary value to fix it.

Let's use an example:

- Your security deposit was $1,000.
- They're only giving you $200 because they said you ruined the carpet with a stain.

That's ludicrous. Carpet cleaning shouldn't be more than a couple hundred dollars. Ask for photos of the carpet and a receipt for the carpet fix (cleaners, replacement, whatever they said they did). You can then negotiate a fair deposit refund. If the building's management can't supply it, it's likely because they used a Tide pen to fix the stain but still want to charge you.

Did you make any attempts to fix the things they're mentioning? If they're saying you stained the carpet, can you provide a carpet-cleaning bill?

If that fails, and you truly did leave the place in perfect condition but they refuse to give you back your money, you can send an email (not a phone call or text) to your landlord saying, "This is my final attempt to work with you directly on the issue of my security deposit refund. I hope we can work this out directly but if not, I'm preparing the documents I have as evidence to file with the county's small claims court."

Emails like this tend to motivate landlords to pay, since they don't want to have to deal with courts. If they still deny you a refund, file with small claims court. They're likely hoping you're bluffing, but if it's important enough to you to get the refund, you can prove you're serious by filing a claim.

Eventually, you have to decide if this money is worth your time. If you're sending a few emails back and forth for $2,000, sure, that's probably worth it. If you're now filing in small claims court over a dispute of $300, maybe it's time to let it go.

If all your attempts fail, just say fuck it and go live your best life. You'll make more money in the future. Just be happy you moved out of their shitty place.

PART TWO

RELATIONSHIP SHIT

HAVE THE COURAGE TO
FALL IN LOVE

Fairytales suck. Every fairytale should have to come with the same disclaimer as true crime reenactments: *This is a dramatization.* Love doesn't happen that way at all.

Here's how fairytales work. You find someone, you fall in love, and you live happily ever after. Nowhere in that bullshit does it mention the courage and empathy it takes to fall in love.

Even the phrase "fall in love" sounds like it's something that happens to you. Like oops, I tripped on the sidewalk and fell in love. Nope. Sorry. Love is a choice. It's waking up each day and choosing the person next to you despite your mood, your infatuation level with them, or how stinky their breath is.

Esther Perel, a badass psychotherapist and genius author, said during one of her TedTalks that "[love is] a verb. It's an active engagement with all kinds of feelings—positive ones and primitive ones and loathsome ones. But it's a very active verb. And it's often surprising how it can kind of ebb and flow. It's like the moon. We think it's disappeared, and suddenly it shows up again. It's not a permanent state of enthusiasm."

She's 100% right. Love is active. Being in love isn't something you wake up with one day and then keep forever.

Being in love is insanely vulnerable. You're walking up to a person, ripping open your chest, exposing your heart, and asking them not to stab it. It takes courage to give someone the ability to know you completely and to crush you undeniably. You're allowing another human being to see parts of you that you often keep hidden from the world. You're showing your flaws to someone and expecting that person to still be there when you do.

So be brave. Take the leap. If you've found a person you feel courageous enough to let love you and you them, fucking go for it. I really do think the old cliché that it's "better to have loved and lost than never to have loved at all" is true. It means you took a risk. You opened yourself up to a possibility of something wonderfully magical, and even if it didn't work out, you grew from it. You now know how great it feels to be in love, to be vulnerable and open with another person. You've proven to yourself that you can love and be loved. Just like the moon, your chance will come around again.

When it comes to love, there's really only one thing you can do.

Love fearlessly.

"IT TAKES COURAGE TO LOVE, BUT PAIN THROUGH LOVE IS THE PURIFYING FIRE WHICH THOSE WHO LOVE GENEROUSLY KNOW. WE ALL KNOW PEOPLE WHO ARE SO MUCH AFRAID OF PAIN THAT THEY SHUT THEMSELVES UP LIKE CLAMS IN A SHELL AND, GIVING OUT NOTHING, RECEIVE NOTHING AND THEREFORE SHRINK UNTIL LIFE IS A MERE LIVING DEATH."

— ELEANOR ROOSEVELT

FALL IN LOVE WITH WHO SOMEONE IS NOW

There's a part in Elizabeth Gilbert's *Eat, Pray, Love* where she talks about how she's fallen in love "with the highest potential of a man, rather than with the man himself...waiting for the man to ascend to his own greatness." Oh, Liz. Me too, girl. Me too.

I've been guilty, on several occasions, of loving someone for their potential. I find myself seeing beyond the person standing in front of me to a false narrative of who that person could be.

I hold people to high expectations because I expect them to do for me what I would do for them. Not all people are built that way. I've had to learn from experience that the person standing before me may be the only version of that person I'll ever see, and to expect from them exactly what they are offering.

If you're in a relationship with someone who says, "I will do ____," or, "I want to be ____," but is taking no action to actually do those things or be those things, believe the person in front of you rather than their words.

This can be particularly hard in romantic relationships because when you love someone you imagine a life with them. You imagine the people you'll become as you grow together. Unfortunately, what you're doing is seeing a mirage of a person in the future without accounting for the person in the present. Perhaps they'll become the person you imagine they'll be, but if they don't, you're to blame for your own disappointment. Not everyone is capable of a glow up.

Falling in love with someone's potential is imagining the dinner they'll make just by staring at the ingredients. It's not your job to hand them the recipe, and if you stand over their shoulder while they cook, they'll just end up resenting you. What happens to your relationship when they take those ingredients and make a totally different meal? What happens if it doesn't taste as good as you imagined it would? Will you still want a seat at the table?

This principle goes beyond romantic relationships. If an employee talks about taking on more responsibility and eventually becoming eligible for that promotion you've been eyeing them for but is uninterested every time you try to hand them something new, believe their actions. If a friend is saying they're sorry they cancel on most of your plans and they want to get better at being reliable, yet they continue to flake out, believe their actions.

So how can you avoid being blinded by your own idealistic vision? First, know your worth and don't settle for less than what you deserve. If you're settling for the person someone is now with the hopes that they'll meet your expectations down the road, you're bound to cause yourself future pain.

Next, don't breeze past the red flags. If something is bothering you in a relationship, don't wait for it to magically fix itself later or for that person to grow into who you want them to be. Sit down and have an honest conversation with them about what bothers you now. Give them the opportunity to change, but if a good amount of time passes and they haven't, it might be time to accept that they aren't the right fit in your life.

Lastly, fall in love with who *you* are now. Stop thinking, "Once I lose ten pounds, then I'll be awesome," or "Once I get the perfect partner or job, then I'll have the life that I love." You're amazing right now. The people and opportunities meant for you will come along in their own time. Don't be hard on yourself because you aren't exactly the person you've envisioned you'd become. I'm certain that the person you already are is pretty great.

If you fall in love with who you are now, others will, too.

DISCERN WHAT'S REALLY LOVE

Being in love is great, isn't it? I have a close friend who jokes about how she's addicted to love. She isn't. She addicted to the feeling of falling in love with someone. She gets so intense with the person she's dating that the rest of the world falls away.

It seems that the love label gets put on a ton of things that aren't love. These things play dress-up and look like love, but they're imposters. I'm talking about lust, infatuation, and limerence.

Lust, where you're drawn to a person like a magnet, can look at lot like a passionate love but once you take a look beneath the surface, you'll usually find there isn't much beyond desire there.

Infatuation, lust's more committal cousin, sees beyond pure passion and finds an intense connection with someone. But it often fizzles out quickly, once the newness of the relationship wears off and comfortability set in.

Limerence is when you're obsessively infatuated with someone, blinded by your desire for them and your need to have a close, intense romantic connection with them. Basically, fireworks! It's that feeling when you first meet someone, you're insanely attracted to them, you think they're perfect, and they can do no wrong. You're ready to move in, elope, and raise their babies within a week of knowing them. Limerence is more rooted in loving and caring feelings than lust, and it lasts longer than infatuation.

Limerence is often associated with addictions or a biochemical reaction—think more obsession than starry-eyed wonder, but I believe it's broader than that. It's overlooking the flaws in a person or in your relationship with them for the much preferred, idealized version of what they, or it, could be. It's sacrificing yourself to ensure the other person wants you in every conceivable way.

Unfortunately, this fake love doesn't last. It can't, because its basis is unsustainable. Either one person is under the puppy love spell and the other person runs from them, or both people are, and with the speed of fireworks, the flame burns out. The trap most people fall into is believing that these passionate experiences are actually love and when they inevitably fade, they think they've fallen *out* of love. If your relationship has a strong core within it, once the infatuation fades, love will be what carries you forward.

People prone to *fast-and-fizzle* relationships are often called "hopeless romantics." If this sounds like you, try to recognize the connection for what it is the next time you feel as though you're being swept off your feet. What is it about this person, and more importantly, this relationship, that's making you feel this way? Is it the core of the person and everything you truly have together? Or is it purely the idea of them and the thought of being in love that you find so intoxicating?

I, myself, have been in relationships where it was hard to distinguish if what I was feeling was true love or infatuation. True love doesn't falter, though. It stays past the honeymoon phase and through the flaws the other person has exposed of themselves.

If you want to know what's really love, write. Write down all of the things about the object of your affection that you know to be true and not fantasy. Write down the ways they treat you. How much of what you feel about this person is actually about them and who they are, and how much of it is your fantasized idea of what the relationship is?

All relationships have a honeymoon phase where everything is perfect. When those big feelings start to fade, just be sure to look at the relationship for what it is, instead of what you hoped it would be. Then you'll know the difference between forever love and temporary passion.

Give It A Fucking Shot

- ☐ The next time you're feeling head over heels in love, stop and give yourself a moment to pause.

- ☐ Try to step outside yourself for a moment and see if you really love this person, or if you love the idea of them or the idea of being in a relationship.

- ☐ Write down all the things about your affection towards this person that you know to be absolutely true. Write down how they treat you and the way you feel. Be honest with yourself about how you're truly feeling towards the relationship.

LEARN HOW TO FIGHT

For most of my childhood people told me not to fight. My parents told me, "Don't hit your brother." My teachers told me, "Don't bicker with your classmates." But real life has fights. No one is around us telling us not to have them, so we have to learn how to have them as adults.

Here are a couple of fights you may come across and some tips for how to handle them.

THE COUPLE FIGHT

If you're in a committed relationship, you're going to have to learn how to fight. Your partner is going to piss you off. You're going to piss them off. Despite how perfect you are, there will come a time when you'll do something that will upset them and they'll do the same to you. The thing to remember is that it isn't you vs. them. It's you and them vs. the problem. If you're truly a team, a real partnership, then most fights will be solvable.

If you asked your partner to call you after work to make plans for the weekend and they forgot, instead of texting "WTF. Did you just forget about me existing on Earth?" try, "Checking in to see if you're still down to talk tonight about this weekend." When they do finally call, you can talk about how it hurt your feelings that they didn't keep their word and it would strengthen your relationship if you both kept the promises you made, even the small ones. If you start a conversation at one hundred, you have nowhere to go.

Esther Perel, the incredible relationship guru I mentioned earlier, talks about how this is the first time in history we have expected this much from one person. We expect our significant other to be our lover, our best friend, our confidant, our mentor, our financial partner, and our source of identity. "We look more frequently to our partner to provide the emotional and physical resources that a village or community used to provide," she says.

When you ask someone to be everything for you, they're bound to fall short sometimes. We have to recognize the pressure we put on our partners and know that sometimes we're going to fight because of these expectations. The important thing is that we learn how to have the fight. Always approach the situation with kindness, because you can never un-say something. You can never un-yell "Fuck You" across a living room. You can never take back the time you said their cooking sucked just because they didn't do the dishes when they said they would.

Don't throw things or physically fight. That's one lesson from childhood that applies here. Treat each other with respect, and remember you love this person. Yes, you're mad at them and you're fighting with them, but you're fighting with a person you chose to love. So choose them. Choose the two of you first, and the fight second. I'm not saying don't have the fight, I'm just saying have it in a productive way.

Listen to the little voice inside your head. I've sat next to a boy-friend more times than I can count, spewing in my own internal flames, having internal fights with them (that I always win), only to never let those words come out of my mouth. Being an overthinker, I don't always trust that my thoughts are real. But if the thoughts don't get released and discussed, no water will be doused on the flames. They'll just retreat to a simmer, at the ready to reignite.

It's important to talk about what's bothering you, even if it will cause a fight. If you don't, your unhappiness will only grow, and your relationship's foundation will begin to crack.

If you're with your person, if the good days outweigh the bad ones, and if you want to work on it, then work on it. It takes less effort to fix problems with a loved one than to start over. You'll fight with the next person, too. It's inevitable.

Some fights are big. Bigger than us. If your fight is big, see a couple's therapist. Therapists are on nobody's side. They are like an unbiased referee, and they can mediate to help you and your partner avoid making the big mistakes you can't take back.

Of course, if the mistake or disagreement or obstacle is too big, it's too big. Big fights will sometimes end in you going your separate ways. Knowing when to call a relationship quits takes a lot of strength, too. At the end of it, at least you can say you tried everything you could to make it work.

THE COWORKER FIGHT

You know how earlier I said it's almost inevitable to end up having a work crush because you spend over forty hours a week with these people? The same is true for fighting. You're going to hate someone at some point because they did something to you. For many of us, work's already very stressful. You're working hard, you're in an enclosed space, you're seeing the same people over and over—and you're expecting sunshine and rainbows all the time? Nope. Not going to happen.

So learn how to have the fight. Don't scream in the office. Don't throw staplers at their head. Don't involve other people or turn anyone against the person you're fighting with. Don't gossip in the break room or plan secret meetings without them.

Instead, take a beat, figure out why you're mad, and then broach the subject with that person. If you're mad because they took credit for your idea, write down or rehearse a way to say it that sounds mature and productive, and then approach them with the problem.

You could start with something like, "I don't know if you know this, but in yesterday's meeting you took credit for the presentation that I put together. I really want to work on a team with you and feel it's best if we make sure credit is given to all of the people who put in the work. It made me feel like you didn't value or respect my effort. I want to figure out a solution together, so we don't have a similar issue arise in the future."

See how productive non-stapler-throwing resolutions can be?

If the problem is too big or if you're too nervous to discuss it with your coworker, consider speaking with a supervisor or Human Resources. There are typically protocols in place for just this scenario but if there aren't, find someone you think could be an advocate and ask for their help.

Know that the more people you rope in, the bigger this will become. If you email your five bosses, Human Resources, the CEO, the European division's entire senior staff, and this person's mom, it's going to become bigger than you might want.

Unless you're prepared to walk out of the door of this company, try to avoid tensions as much as possible while still making sure your voice is heard and your problem is made clear with the intent to resolve it quickly.

THE FAMILY FIGHT

Family is tough. We don't choose them. Even if we're talking about in-laws, we chose the person, not their family. Sure, you can block your racist uncle from Facebook but that won't make Thanksgiving less awkward. Families fight all the time. It's the basis for about half of all reality TV. So how do you handle the real family fights—the ones that cause rifts for generations?

I really wish there was a clear-cut answer to that. Every family dynamic is different, and each fight is different. The important thing to remember is that these people, whether you want them or not, are yours. You didn't choose them, but you also can't erase them forever (well, not easily).

I've found that with family, the best approach is direct. Don't sugar coat it, but don't be harsh. It's okay to say, "You did this thing and it really hurt my feelings. I love you but we have to figure out a way to work this out." Similar to the couple fight, if you approach it as if you're on the same team, things may get resolved faster. Try not to rope in everyone here, either—your third cousin's wife doesn't care that your mother embarrassed you in front of your friends. However, your immediate family might, and if a fight is about something habitual, it might be worth bringing in siblings or other people to say, "We've noticed a pattern and we need to address it before it escalates."

If the fight is decades-long, it might be time to let that person go. We're stuck with family in a certain way, but as we grow older, family becomes more of a choice. Ever since the invention of caller ID, we've had the option of who we talk to. Fight for the family that you see in your future but let go of the ones who cause you more harm than good.

THE BEST FRIEND FIGHT

So you found a person at nineteen who's your ride or die. You're going to go to every event together, celebrate every birthday together and die next to each other at one-hundred-years-old with martinis in hand. Sure. But it's a long time before you reach one-hundred-years-old, so you're going to fight. Learn how.

Best friend relationships can be super delicate. A lot of the same advice from the couple fight section still applies, but also remember that for some people, friendships are easier to walk away from than romantic relationships, and for other people, they're harder to walk away from. That doesn't mean you should approach a fight with your best friend differently—it just means that you have to recognize your own investment in the relationship.

Life is really hard and all the fights above are going to happen—it's important to have your best friend by your side when they do. Just remember—your best friend has been there for all the other fights. When your lover cheats on you, when you're not speaking to your father, or when your coworker makes a snide comment, best friends are the ones who get you through it.

SEARCH FOR WHAT'S BELOW THAT

I was talking with a friend who told me that she'd been fighting a lot with her boyfriend and they weren't getting anywhere. She felt like they were having the same fight over and over again. I asked her what they were fighting about, and she said it was "silly things," like one of them being messy or disagreeing about who is pitching in more.

I related hard to that. I've been in relationships where I felt like we were having the same fight constantly and not getting a resolution.

I learned a tool from my therapist I call, "What's Below That?" Here's how it works.

THE PROBLEM
I feel like I'm cleaning more than you.

THE FIGHT
Both people feel like they're doing more than the other person and are trying to one up each other on who contributes more.
This is usually where the fight would get stuck in a loop and end unresolved.

WHAT'S BELOW THAT LAYER
I feel like I try harder than you.

NEW PROBLEM
You're not trying in this relationship.

WHAT'S BELOW THAT LAYER
I feel like you don't care about me as much as I care about you.

NEW PROBLEM
You don't show me you care about me as much as I need.

Okay, now you have something tangible to work on. In what ways do you need someone to show they care? In what ways do you think you show them that you care? Talk about the ways you like to be cared for and ways you like to care for others. See if your styles and methods of caring are compatible, and if not, address how you can work on them together to give each other what you need.

If you can't figure out how to get at "What's Below That?" ask your basic questions from first grade: Who? What? Where? When? Why?

WHO?
Who am I really annoyed at? Am I really mad at my partner, or is this something else from another part of my day coming up?

WHAT?
What exactly is bothering me? What is the emotion I'm feeling? What causes this reaction in me?

WHERE?
Where in my body do I feel this? Is it in my gut? Is it in my heart? Is it in my head?

WHEN?
When do these problems seem to arise? Is there a pattern to the timing, like after a night out, or at the end of the week when we're exhausted?

WHY?
Why does this hurt? Why am I annoyed? Why do I feel this way?

Keep going until you feel like you've hit the last layer. Something usually clicks in you when you've reached it, like, "Oh shit. That feels really right. That's the final layer for sure." It's like a realization moment for both of you.

You may not hit the bottom layer the first time. Your first "What's Below That?" fight may still result in a similar conversation later that reveals a layer deeper.

Take the problem above. It may not end at, "I feel like you don't care about me as much as I care about you." It may go further into, "I feel like you don't value me as a partner," or, "I feel like you don't respect my contribution to this relationship." It doesn't have to be that deep, though. It's possible that talking about how to care for each other is the final layer and those other layers aren't relevant to your relationship. It's also possible your partner doesn't show that they care in the ways you need but that you do feel valued and respected by them.

Go with your gut. If you dig into a layer that doesn't feel like it clicks with this problem, then that's probably not the area you need to explore. You can keep digging, but don't dig so far down that you begin to generate problems that aren't there to begin with. It might not be a layer deeper, it might be at the same level as "you don't care as much about me as I do about you," but a different problem such as "the ways you show you care for me make me feel unneeded."

Keep peeling back the layers to find what the actual problem is.

Just know that your approach is key. Bring up problems with your partner as calmly as possible so that you can find out "What's Below That?" together, while avoiding a screaming match.

Give It A Fucking Shot

☐ Start with your current problem and fight. If you aren't sure how to word it, try writing it down. Keep it short—one or two sentences.

☐ Take a step back, possibly take a walk or listen to some music, and think (calmly), "What's really going on here?". Not what's on the surface, but what's below it.

☐ If you aren't getting an answer, try your who, what, where, when and why questions to get you there.

☐ Keep peeling back layers until an answer clicks. You'll know it when you get there.

☐ Work through that layer with your partner and see if the resolution that comes about brings an end to the formerly repetitive fights.

STOP KEEPING SCORE

Your roommate, brother, girlfriend, whoever, pissed you off. You paid for the last two grocery runs and they didn't even offer. You cleaned the dishes the past six times and they made just as many dirty dishes as you did. You bought them a $200 holiday present and they bought you a $14 coffee mug.

Stop keeping score. Here's what you didn't see.

They've been struggling recently and some days just putting on pants is hard. They don't have the energy to go to the grocery store. They barely have the energy to go to the kitchen.

They wiped down the sink after you did dishes, did a load of laundry, and made the bed. They brought in the mail. They picked up a spoon you left on the coffee table and put it in the sink on their way out of the door. They did things you weren't conscious of because it had slipped your mind. Dishes may have slipped theirs.

They don't have the money right now to buy you a fancy holiday gift because they had an unexpected expense come up. You didn't see the two hours they spent online scrolling through endless coffee mugs to pick out the one that would make you smile.

We get so caught up in what we did that we tend not to notice what the other person did. I once heard that when you feel like you're doing 90% of the work in a relationship, you're really doing 50%. We're blind to the things the other person is doing because we're so in our head about the things we're doing. Step outside yourself to notice the little things.

Imbalances can happen. Life gets in the way of a perfectly balanced relationship. One person gets busier than the other. One person has different obstacles than the other. Calmly approach the subject in a mature manner and have a solid conversation.

Say things like:

> "I know you've been busy recently, but I feel like things in the house have gotten a bit messy and I'd love it if we could divide and tackle some of the chores."

> "I just saw the cutest shirt online. If you ever need a gift for me, this is perfect."

> "I just want you to know that I notice when you do little things around the house and it makes me feel loved."

Positive reinforcement of the small things often motivates people to do more. Negative feedback can make people retreat behind a wall of resentment. If you're feeling like you're pulling more than your weight, consider approaching it from a place of acknowledgment for the things they are doing while still addressing what you would like to add to the relationship.

Nothing is ever perfectly even or perfectly balanced. There will be times when you need to take a break and kick your feet up and there will be someone there to help. That's how humanity works. We take care of each other.

Come at the conversation with an open mind. It's not about what you do for others. If you want to keep people in your life, focus on the relationship before the scorecard.

Give It A Fucking Shot

☐ Throw away the scorecard and think of five things the other person has done for you recently.

☐ If you can't think of five things they've done for you, think of five things *someone* has done for you recently when you didn't do the same for them.

CHOOSE EACH OTHER

You don't say, "I love you" once and then know you'll just be in love forever. Love is choosing the other person every day. It's waking up and looking at the other person and saying, "I see your flaws, all of them, and still I choose you."

Relationships take work. Like a lot of work. That's why there are entire sections in bookstores dedicated to making relationships work. Lifestyle websites have entire divisions devoted to giving relationship advice.

We've touched on this in a few other chapters but let's dive into it a bit deeper. Every day may not be heaven on earth. Love is still choosing the person on tough days—days that test your relationship.

After a fight, when you're ready to walk out of the relationship, you have to make a choice. If you want this person, you have the choice to stay. There are definitely fights I've had that have ended relationships and my friends will say, "Why didn't you just work through that?" The pure answer: we stopped choosing each other. The same is true for my friend's relationships. They'll break up with someone and I'll think, "Oh, if I really wanted to be with that person, I would've made that work." The truth is, we all make different choices.

Let's look at Bill and Hillary Clinton for a moment. I know. Blast from the past. If you're old enough to remember it, when the Monica Lewinsky scandal broke, people were very split on how Hillary should handle it. It was either, "She should dump his ass. I can't believe she's even standing near him in these press meetings," or,

"She loves him, and they worked so hard to get to the White House. I bet they can work past this."

Of course, it's only up to the two of them on how to proceed. Bill and Hillary decided to make it work, but that was their choice. You always have a choice. You even have choices within those choices. Hillary likely said, "I'll stay, but we have to figure out how to proceed in this relationship. That was really uncool, Bill." (Okay, I wasn't there but that's how I imagine the conversation went.)

Hard choices can be an opportunity to redefine previously gray areas. Maybe for Bill, the things one should and should not do in the Oval Office were a gray area. Now there's a roadmap for similar situations based on the choices Bill made in this instance.

Make plans when you're happy for times when you're not. For example, if you're dating a recovering addict, have the discussion about what you would do if they relapsed. It's going to be much harder to have that conversation and to make a choice in the moment with all the heightened emotions flying around. It doesn't mean you're bound to the choice, of course, because every situation is different. But if you have the conversation ahead of time, then you both have an idea of how things will play out. You could say, "If you ever relapsed and hid it from me, I would leave. But if you relapsed and told me so we could seek help together, I think we could work through that."

That's you setting your boundaries and acknowledging your anticipated choice. Know that if the time comes to actually make the choice, you could feel differently, but at least you have laid the groundwork. You're not starting from zero.

Every moment you are with your partner is a choice. It's the choice to be together.

Every breakup is a choice. One or both of you have chosen not to be together.

"THE WRONG ONE WILL FIND
YOU IN PEACE AND LEAVE
YOU IN PIECES, BUT THE
RIGHT ONE WILL FIND YOU
IN PIECES AND LEAD YOU TO
PEACE."

— UNKNOWN

SURVIVE A BREAKUP OR DIVORCE

When we're little, we're taught we'll grow up, find our perfect person, and live happily ever after. What they forget to tell us is there will be a lot of relationships where this doesn't happen. You're going to have your heart broken a ton of times.

Unfortunately, these times often occur when you have other shit going on. You have to keep going to work, you have to still go on that vacation with the family, you still have to attend your friend's wedding. How do you keep life moving when you want the world to just pause so you can heal?

I've been there. Here are the things that help me.

WRITING

I have found writing to be extremely helpful. Write your thoughts and feelings in a journal. You can even purchase "breakup journals" with guided prompts to help you get started. Write down a list of reasons why that person isn't right for you or that relationship isn't good for you. Write down what you learned from the experience to help you move forward. Write a letter to your future or past self, describing what the experience meant to you.

Don't write to the person you've broken up with. You can write down the things you WOULD say to them but don't send it. Keep your power. Don't reach out or you give it away. They don't deserve to hear from you, anyways. When they lost you, they lost all of you.

No good comes from seeking healing in the place that broke you. Heal yourself before you reach out (if you must reach out at all).

FRIEND SUPPORT

Call friends and talk it through. Anytime you want to text the ex, text a friend instead. They're there to support and love you. If that's not an option, text a family member or chat online with a professional.

BE ACTIVE

Go on an adventure, drive to the beach to clear your head, go for a hike. Short on time? Go for a twenty-minute walk to get fresh air. Moving your body helps a lot. Go for a run, even if you don't usually run. Take it slow but let the endorphins rush through your veins and clear your mind.

WATCH MOVIES

This can be the perfect way to re-center yourself, and there's nothing wrong with sitting on the couch for hours on end and watching movies that bring you comfort. Eat some yummy foods while you're at it. Just relax and enjoy something comforting. Some of my favorites are *First Wives Club*, *Eat Pray Love*, *How to Be Single*, *When Harry Met Sally*, *Forgetting Sarah Marshall*, and *Girls Trip*. There are so many fantastic movies out there to help you through this time. Watch TV shows that you loved as a kid or in college. It's been proven that watching shows you've seen before can calm anxiety, because you already know the outcome.

READ INSPIRATIONAL AND MOTIVATIONAL QUOTES

I actually made a Pinterest board after a breakup of quotes I found useful, and now resort back to it when needed. Here are a few from anonymous sources to get you started:

> "The person who broke you can't be the one to fix you. Remember that."

> "If someone truly loves you, they won't be in a position to lose you."

"I don't know who needs to hear this, but they were never going to change. You did the right thing."

"Life is like a book. Some chapters are sad. Some are happy. Some are exciting. But if you never turn the page, you will never know what the next chapter holds."

"Little reminder. Choose the people who choose you."

"I would rather adjust my life to your absence than adjust my value to your disrespect."

"Just because a decision hurts doesn't mean it was the wrong decision."

"It's okay if you thought you were over it, but it hits you all over again. It's okay to fall apart even if you thought you had it under control. You're not weak. Healing is messy. And there's no timeline for healing."

"Fuck. Them. I deserve better."

MAKE A KILLER PLAYLIST AND BLAST IT

I have a playlist called "Move Forward" that's made up of songs that inspire me to do just that. They aren't sappy songs about how amazing that person was, but rather songs about how amazing I am. Everyone has their own music choices but here are a few of my favorites.

I'm Still Standing - Elton John

You Don't Own Me - Lesley Gore

Truth Hurts - Lizzo

Not Today - Alessia Cara

IDGAF - Dua Lipa (or really any of her songs—she nails this topic. New Rules. Don't Start Now.)

B.O.M.O - Tatiana Manaois

Irreplaceable - Beyoncé (or Best Thing I Never Had)

Too Good At Goodbyes - Sam Smith

Someone Like You - Adele

Thank You, Next - Ariana Grande

Back To Black - Amy Winehouse

Hell, blasting "Burn" from the Hamilton soundtrack works, too. Now go dance that ass off. You'll get the added bonus of a nice revenge body if you dance for hours on end.

AVOID SOCIAL MEDIA
Don't stalk your ex on social media. Full stop. Nothing good comes from this. It's like picking at a scab, you're going to bleed and nothing will happen to them. If you need to log out of your social media accounts on all of your devices to control this habit, do it.

LISTEN TO PODCASTS
I love listening to podcasts or Ted Talks. Brené Brown and Dan Savage are awesome for these moments.

REMOVE THIS PERSON FROM YOUR PHONE AND COMPUTER
This can mean uploading photos of you two to the cloud and removing them from your phone. This can be as small as removing their

address from Postmates. Slowly, go through each of your apps and remove them. If you aren't ready to delete the text chain, save that for another day. Do something smaller today, like deleting their phone number from your favorites. If you have family pictures with them in it, there are plenty of apps out there to edit their face out.

SEEK THERAPY

Whether you have someone you see regularly or have never gone to therapy before, it's good to have someone who's on your side, who doesn't know your ex, and who is there to support you emotionally. You can see them in person, virtually, or even by phone.

This is especially important if you're going through a divorce and are struggling with custody or divorce proceedings. That's a lot to carry; let someone else help you carry it.

BREATHE

There are going to be good days and bad days. Good moments and bad moments. It's a rollercoaster of the stages of grief. Within an hour you could be super angry, super sad, and super lonely. Just breathe and know it's all okay. Everything passes.

TAKE THE TIME YOU NEED

You're a great employee, a wonderful friend, an incredible person— it's okay to take the time you need. Take a day off from work if you need it; you'll make it up when you're feeling better. Cancel that dinner party plan to stay home. It's okay to take care of you.

Time heals all wounds. I promise.

ACKNOWLEDGE MOST RELATIONSHIPS END

Dan Savage, host of the *Savage Lovecast*, says, "Every relationship you are in will fail, until one doesn't." Quite the uplifting note for a chapter to start on, right? It's true, though. All of your romantic relationships in your life will end except one; the last one. Want to know what's crazier? You're never *really* sure if the one you're in right now is the last one. You aren't dead yet, so it might not be.

You can only see so far into the future, but my guess is you might already have an inkling about whether or not your current relationship is the last one or not. Regardless, you shouldn't write off any relationship as a failure just because it might not be your last one. Most relationships will come in and out of your life in the time they're meant to. It's the mark they leave on you that will last a lifetime.

Why do we believe that when it comes to love, it's either 100% or 0%? If the person you're with isn't the love of your life, your be-all-end-all, then you're supposed to think they are some mistake. If a relationship ends, it doesn't mean that you have to chalk that relationship up (or down) to a zero.

Just because it didn't last forever doesn't mean it wasn't meaningful or important. If you were with someone for six months, and the last month was rough and that's what led to the breakup, that's an overall good relationship. Five wonderful months means 83% of that relationship was great. It's four out of five stars. LeBron James had a 69% free throw percentage in the 2019-2020 season, and he's considered one of the greatest basketball players of all time.

If you learned something from the person you were in a relationship with, or from that relationship in general, congratulations—that was worth it. If you grew as a person and now have wonderful memories, that was worth it. You were likely right for each other during the time you were together and just because you didn't continue to be right for each other forever doesn't mean the relationship failed and should now be erased from history—it means you changed. It's rare that someone defines change or growth in a person as failure. Why do it in a relationship?

When you look back on relationships from your past, accept them for what they were. You don't have to smile fondly at the memories, but know that the bang-up, incredible person you are today is because of these experiences. You're not a failure. Neither are the relationships that led you to become this person. They just weren't 100% successful. You're amazing no matter how many relationships you've walked away from.

The most important relationship you have is with you. That one, I guarantee, lasts a lifetime.

LEAVE FOR YOUR REASONS

At the end of my longest relationship, I told my friends that "I wish he had just cheated." It would absolve me of the guilt I felt for leaving for what seemed like no reason. I wasn't happy anymore. I hadn't been for over a year and I had been considering leaving for many months at that point, but I wanted there to be a reason. Something horrible that one of us, preferably him, had done to make it easier to explain to people. Something that sounded better than, "I just wasn't in it anymore." I no longer wanted to choose him as my person.

It took a long time and a few shorter relationships after that to know that being unhappy is enough of a reason. So is no reason at all, but rather a gut feeling. Sometimes things just don't work out. If you're hunting for a reason to leave, that's your reason. When you start asking friends how they knew when it was time to end a relationship, or you start searching online for reasons to break up, that's your reason.

It doesn't have to be a grand dramatic reason or one that's socially acceptable to everyone because they've seen it a million times before in movies. It doesn't matter what anyone else thinks or even if anyone else knows.

I don't usually tell people the reason a relationship ended for the simple fact that they don't need to know. It wasn't their relationship that ended, so why does it matter if they know the reason? People will always think they are entitled to the reason, but you don't have to give it to them. That's their issue, not yours. I've gotten very good at deflecting with responses like, "There were a lot of reasons we ended the relationship," or, "That's really between us and I don't feel comfortable discussing that with you."

The truth is, there often isn't just one reason a relationship ends, there are usually a ton of reasons. It's usually a very layered situation that led you to wanting to leave and defining it in one sentence can be tough.

Even if someone cheats, you may have already been drifting apart. If one person in a relationship becomes neglectful, emotionally distant, and unwilling to work on the issues at hand and the other person cheats, we as a culture always say, "Well, that's the bad guy. The one who cheated has to be the bad guy." We completely discredit all of the things that might have led up to the infidelity.

I had always thought there had to be a huge, indisputable reason for ending a relationship, but there doesn't have to be. You can leave for the simple reason that you want to and that you see no other way towards happiness. That's enough.

GET YOUR HEART BROKEN

Admit it. You opened up to this chapter, read the title, and were like, "What the fuck? This lady's crazy." You're right. I am, but that's not the point here.

The point is that you need to get your heart broken. Probably a few times. Like, seriously broken. Shattered. Ripped out of your chest, stomped on, and flattened.

That's how you get clarity.

I had a boyfriend in high school who liked to cheat on me like it was his career aspiration. Like he was training for the Fucking Olympics. Not the fucking Olympics, but the Olympics of Fucking. I didn't matter. I loved him. Well, I thought I did. He was my high school puppy love. We dated for almost two years. He was a football player, with dirty blonde hair and huge biceps. We broke up almost a year into that relationship when I found out about the first time he cheated. Holy shit, I was devastated. I could hardly stand up. I couldn't look at him, I couldn't think about him without feeling a wave of anxiety rush through my body. He convinced me it wasn't true, and I took him back. What can I say? I was young and he was my first real boyfriend. We dated for another eight or nine months and he started acting weird again. I left him for good this time and found out about more of the young ladies he was running around with, but you know what? It didn't matter anymore. He couldn't hurt me like he did before because the person he broke didn't exist anymore.

I wish I could tell you that was the only time my heart was shattered, but it wasn't. People haven't been particularly careful with it and to be honest, I think a few of them might have decided to use it for batting practice.

You know what happens after you get your heart broken? You rebuild. Except this time, you're laying different bricks. You're no longer built from material that says you'll tolerate someone who treats you that way. You're stronger than the last time. You'll have a much better foundation beneath you. You are a fucking brick house.

Every time I had my heart broken, I learned more about myself. I learned what I deserve and what I definitely don't deserve. I learned what I needed in a relationship. How I want to be treated. I learned the value of my support system and grew closer to my friends through experiencing heartbreak.

You learn that you won't die. That you can survive heartbreak. You learn to adjust to a change in vision. You saw your life going one way, with one specific person and then things shift so you learn to shift with them.

You learn how to heal. I mean really heal. Not "brush past it because it didn't mean that much, anyways" kind of healing, but deep healing. The kind you can only do when you've hit bottom. I've spent plenty of time getting up, dusting myself off, pushing past any uncomfortable feelings and boldly saying, "I'm fine," when I wasn't. Deep healing comes when you learn how to sit in your feelings, work through them, love yourself, and move forward stronger than before.

Heartbreak forces you to become a new and improved version of yourself. You learn your value. You learn how to show others what that value is and prove you don't offer discounts. Trust me, I've put myself on a Black Friday sale more times than I care to admit. You don't need to compromise yourself to be with someone else, but oftentimes the only way to really learn that is through heartbreak.

Eventually, you won't fear losing someone so much that you ignore their flaws. You'll know that if you lost them, you'll still be standing just as strong as you were before they entered your life.

I wish there was a better way. I really do. If there is, tell me. For now, all I know is it takes devastation to receive clarity and grow from it.

Give It A Fucking Shot

- ☐ Just kidding. (But if you do get your heart broken, know you'll survive it).

BE YOUR OWN "PERSON"

A few months after separating from my ex-partner, I was visiting a new doctor and they handed me some introductory paperwork. The standard stuff, insurance information, address—nothing crazy.

Then I got to the bottom of the form and paused. Emergency Contact. He had been my emergency contact on every form for most of my adult life. Who do I put now? My parents? I was in my late twenties and something about adding my parents felt wrong. I did it anyway because I had about thirty seconds to complete this form and blanked on people I knew. My best friend was a solid runner-up, but I didn't feel comfortable putting her in that kind of position in case something *did* happen.

My real crisis was that I didn't have a "person" anymore. That unquestionable fallback person for any emergency or crisis. Who was going to drive me to the emergency room if something happened? Who was going to come pick me up if my car broke down on the side of the road? I had always thought of myself as an incredibly independent person until this moment when I realized I had relied heavily on someone else for some pretty major stuff.

I started making a plan.

Who was going to drive me to the emergency room? An ambulance. A friend. An Uber. Myself if possible.

Who was going to pick me up if my car broke down? AAA. A friend. My parents. Again, an Uber. Those things are handy.

Unfortunately, in life, shit happens. By planning these scenarios, I became my own person. I no longer had a giant question mark over these moments. Having a plan just let me relax a little bit in knowing that I'll be fine. I can handle whatever crap life wants to throw at me and I don't need to depend on someone else to be my "person."

No one's going to be all things for you. Be your own person.

Give It A Fucking Shot

☐ Think of a few scenarios where you might need someone's help. Examples might include anything you would need insurance for (car accident, health emergency).

☐ Then, make a plan of two or three ways you could handle that. You want a backup in case plan A doesn't go... well, according to plan.

END YOUR SEARCH FOR THE PERFECT PERSON

Do you own a single item in your home that's perfect? I don't. When I bought my car, I was convinced it was perfect. Then, within the first week, I noticed it had a blind spot off the driver's side and my dog's hair would get caught in between the backseat and the buckle, making it extra hard to clean.

My favorite sweater that I wear all the time has a weird seam issue on the bottom-right side of it. I love it. It's still my favorite sweater, but it's flawed.

Remember every magical vacation you've had? Did it rain one day? Did a piece of your luggage get lost? Did you have a major zit on your face that caused you to adjust every photo you took to hide it? Does any of that matter? When you think back on it now, don't you remember the good shit instead of the bad shit?

Nothing is perfect. Why do we assume a person is going to be perfect, let alone perfect for us? I'm not perfect, yet I'm expecting someone else to be? There can't possibly be a perfect person, because everyone defines perfect differently. For me, a "perfect" partner is just someone that has my non-negotiable qualities—honest, caring, adventurous, and a good sense of humor.

Since you can't have a perfect person, you can't have a perfect relationship. There will always be flaws. You may have found a great person who leaves clothing all over the floor or who's always on their phone when you watch TV. This can be super annoying, but it's just proof that the person, and the relationship, aren't perfect.

They're better than perfect—they're real. Now it's up to you to decide if it's right for you. If it's not, then end the relationship, list out your non-negotiables, and don't give up until you find someone who checks all of those boxes. If you decide to stick with your imperfect person, you have to let those things go.

Accept what's in front of you or go stand somewhere else.

I know this might be hard to swallow, but everyone has flaws and so do you. I'm sure there are things about you that your partner has learned to accept. That's the nature of the game. Dating isn't finding the perfect person; it's finding the person who's perfect for us.

If you haven't found that person yet, keep looking. To someone out there in the world, you're perfect.

"AND NOW THAT YOU DON'T HAVE TO BE PERFECT, YOU CAN BE GOOD."

— JOHN STEINBECK

VALIDATE YOURSELF

I know this sounds super cheesy. It's one of the most popular clichés in the world – happiness comes from within. You're probably envisioning it embroidered on a throw pillow right now. It's also unarguably accurate.

No one else is ever going to make you happy. You have to make you happy.

No one is ever going to show you who you are and what you are capable of. Only you can do that.

I once dated a guy who went from relationship to relationship. He couldn't be alone for more than a few days; he constantly had to be around friends, roommates, or a significant other, and couldn't be single for more than a week or two between relationships. When our relationship ended, he rushed to find someone else and got into a new relationship within a few weeks. I had learned from the stories of his past relationships that he was hardly ever single, mostly because he would date a few people and then attach himself to the one he liked enough to spend his time with.

I suppose his behavior could've been defined by a term like "serial monogamist," but to me what it came down to was a fear of being alone. Not just physically alone, but alone with only his own thoughts. He had a fear of feeling inadequate or unhappy because of a lack of external validation.

What I noticed from his behavior is that he didn't know who he was, and was seeking validation from someone else. If someone else liked him, then he was fine the way he was—no need to dig any deeper. He was seeking happiness from people on the outside rather than working to find happiness on the inside.

He always explained the end of his relationships by saying, "I realized I didn't like this person," or, "I felt things had changed." What he was really saying was, "They stopped validating me the way I want."

When we put the onus on others to complete us, we will forever be incomplete.

When we expect others to change us, we will never actually change.

When we are unhappy, the only way out is to discover the things inside ourselves that bring us happiness. I told you it sounds cheesy, but it's true.

It's always wonderful to get compliments and words of affirmation from those who love us. The problem lies with when we begin to place the weight of our own validation, assurance, happiness, and inner peace on others. That's when we're doomed to never truly find those things for ourselves.

This isn't to say if we're having a tough day, we shouldn't pick up the phone and call our friends for support. Of course we should. This also isn't to say that we shouldn't date or seek people to join our lives because we're a work in progress. We will always be a work in progress. You're never done growing.

We just need to make sure that we aren't putting the ownership of our own happiness and mental well-being on others, or more importantly, on how others see us. You're enough and the right people will see that. You don't need anyone's approval.

If you're feeling lonely and you're reaching for your phone to call someone (anyone), pause for a moment and check in with yourself. Breathe into the feeling of loneliness and remind yourself that you're extraordinary, you're capable of creating your own happiness, and you don't need someone else to prove that.

SELECT YOUR DETECTIVE MOMENTS

Remember the boyfriend who cheated on me when I was in high school? Like, cheated on me a lot?

Every woman out there knows that you become a full-blown detective when your intuition pipes up. In high school, I was dead on the money. I found shit no one wishes they knew.

Unfortunately, once you have that habit, it's a hard one to break. I was in a very long relationship, long after the cheating, teenage boyfriend, but still had trust issues. Someone had damaged that part of me, but rather than address it or even notice it existed, I became a detective.

We reached a point where our lives were entangled. We shared passwords to email accounts, shared bank accounts, and sometimes I would find myself digging for something, anything. I didn't know what I was looking for, but somehow, every time I went looking, I'd find something suspicious. I was great at working myself up into a full-blown panic attack because I found a receipt for $16 spent at a coffee shop and figured he must have bought stuff for two people. In these moments the concept that they may also serve food escaped my mind because I acquired temporary tunnel vision.

Once you start employing your spy tactics for little, inconclusive leads, your partner stops trusting you. They begin to think you're paranoid. If you hear alarm bells going off and your gut is saying something is wrong, then it might be. You can rest your finger comfortably on the button to deploy your detective skills but give your partner a chance to tell their side before you press it. Give them the opportunity to explain the $16 coffee bill before you start calling the coffee shop asking for security footage.

If you're snooping, there's a reason. Stop following their footsteps and follow your reason for why you think you have to snoop. There's something deeper going on. If you're truly happy in your relationship and you fully trust your partner, you wouldn't have this desire. There's something being triggered in you that needs to be addressed. Something from a previous relationship could be coming up for you in your current one. Maybe it's something from childhood you didn't even know stuck with you all these years. It could be something from your past you aren't even conscious of. If you think that might be the case, identify what that something is. Start with revisiting the *Search For What's Below That* chapter and seeing if you can dig into the layer that's triggering these tendencies. If you can't seem to find it, therapists are great at helping people get to the bottom of what's bothering them.

Once I began exploring the issues I had, my desire to play detective faded. I've been more comfortable in my relationships since. If similar issues come up in new relationships, I try to find the layer in me that's bringing up those feelings.

So put the phone down, stop trying to guess their childhood pet's birthday as a passcode, and find the deeper root to the problem.

If the deeper root is that you don't trust your partner, address why. It may very well be that they aren't a trustworthy partner or have done something to make you suspicious. In this case, ask to see their phone or email rather than snoop around. Someone without anything to hide will gladly grant you that access without you having to go undercover. Sit beside them so they can answer your questions immediately before you get swept away by minor details.

It's also possible that you don't trust your current partner because a former partner left you with trust issues.

If the deeper root is that you have trust issues in general, address why. Could it be something from childhood that's causing you to distrust people in adulthood? If so, dig into what that could be so you can work through it and finally relax when your partner's phone dings from the other room.

It's often simpler than we think. Start with the *What's Below That* method and see if you can figure it out on your own. The answer could be hiding just one layer below the surface.

GET COMFORTABLE SAYING NO

Boundaries are important. Physical boundaries. Emotional boundaries. Property boundaries to keep the neighbor's annoying kids out. You name the boundary—it matters. Boundaries define how people treat you.

If you're a people pleaser like me, you find setting boundaries difficult. I don't want to make anyone mad because they want to do or say something and my reaction is, "No." My instinct not to be a buzzkill means I find myself in situations I'd rather not be in.

There are the obvious boundaries, like walking away from an unsafe situation. It's easy to say no when your sketchy neighbor asks if you want to go check out his rock collection. Then there are the less obvious boundaries, like asking someone not to talk about a topic that may be triggering for you.

My personal concept for boundaries is simple: I care about others, but I care about me first. If I'm always putting someone else before myself and it's harming my wellbeing, it's time to set some boundaries.

Is someone constantly making you anxious? Are you feeling like you have to compromise yourself to meet someone else's need? Are you stressing yourself out trying to avoid a conversation or situation? Then it's time to set some boundaries.

Boundaries are awesome. Setting boundaries is like making a little "how-to-interact with me" guide. When you set boundaries, you're creating healthy relationships, you're holding others accountable for how they treat you, and you're validating your own needs.

If you're nervous about how to approach boundary-setting conversations, here are some starters:

- I know you're not trying to hurt me, but it bothers me when you do this.
- I respond better, and can actually hear what you're saying, when we approach problems from a calmer place rather than yelling.
- I think my words are being received differently than I intended, let me try to rephrase what I mean.
- Can we please pause this conversation? I need to take a break for a little bit.
- I would love to help you with that, but I need some down time today.
- I'm not ready to share that idea yet but I'll let you know when I am.

The above are kind ways of expressing what you need without hurting others. The best part about these conversation starters is that they don't come across as an outright, "No," but rather a, "Let's work this out." If you need to set some boundaries, don't be afraid and go for it. The people you want in your life will respect how you want to be treated.

MAKE AND MAINTAIN FRIENDSHIPS

Let's talk about how to make adult friends and maintain adult friendships. Chances are, most of your childhood friendships were formed through school or neighborhood interactions. The same is likely true through your early twenties. Then you get out into the world and the world's like, "Good luck. Hope you stayed connected with that girl from sixth grade."

So, how do you make friends as an adult? Maybe you start through friends of friends. If you're active, you'll meet friends through hobbies or traveling. You might even make friends with coworkers. Once you've gotten to know someone well enough in the office, ask them to coffee or lunch one day and voila, friendship born.

You could join a sports club, hobby meetup, networking group, or local class (acting, dance, cooking, language) and meet some awesome people. This is a great strategy because you'll already know that you have a shared interest.

Maybe you're brave and start exploring your city alone. Try meeting people in museums, on hikes, or even when eating alone at a restaurant.

Don't be afraid to walk up to someone and start talking. Channel the six-year-old version of you who once shared crayons and struck up a conversation about your favorite color.

Cool. Now you've got loads of friends.

How do we maintain those friendships once we have them?

As we get older, our world narrows. Our lives get busier and our priorities shift. People get married and have kids, move to a different city, state, or country, and make new friends and the former ones seem to fade into the background.

Friendships can be the through line of your life's story or become a footnote on the final page. When all the other stuff comes into our lives, we must make an effort to maintain the friendships that are important to us. Naturally, we may only hold on to a few people from childhood, maybe a few from high school or college, and some from previous stages of adulthood.

I have a group of three girlfriends who I used to work with about five years ago. We're still very close and while our lives have all shifted drastically, we still make it a point to see each other about once a month. We have a text chain that updates us on each other's lives. We celebrate birthdays and the holidays together. We even take a weekend trip together every now and then.

I have a few close friends in my city that I try to see a few times a year. We have a great time and I put in the effort to make sure I see them often enough that we're a presence in each other's lives. When we get together, it's effortless and feels like no time has passed, even with six months between visits.

I also have a handful of close friends from childhood that I'll text once a month or so to check in. Sometimes a few months go by and I realize I didn't reach out, so I make a quick call. I keep in touch because my friends' presence in my life is important and something I know I don't want to lose.

I also have friends who pop in and out of my life. These are people I've met along the way who I see every now and then. I know that one day they may not be there, but it doesn't change anything from what we've shared. I just know that I can't maintain every friendship in my life.

I have to prioritize the friendships that mean the most to me. The size of your circle doesn't matter. If your personal circle fills your friendship quota, then you're good. Having a few close friends has been more meaningful to me than having a long list of acquaintances.

My prioritized friendships are like a Myspace Top 8 in real time. These are the people who I can call when I've had a long day or need advice. These are the people whose new relationships I want to hear about, who I'm always there to help when they need me, the people I would even go fetch from the airport. Recognizing my personal limits has allowed me to focus on the friendships that I want to sustain for a long time. I still value all of my other friendships for the roles they play in my life, but I know it isn't realistic to try and maintain every friend I've ever had forever.

There's no right way to do friendships. My parents talk about how they invited a handful of friends to their wedding that they never saw again. A wedding guest list should be made up of the people you're closest with, the people you want to share your special day with. Sometimes the people you think will be in your life forever end up walking out of it before you thought they would. They still leave their footprints. There isn't any judgment on how a friendship is supposed to be. All the people who have come in and out of your life have made you the person you are, right now.

Focus on maintaining the relationships you want to hold onto forever but don't feel bad if some friendships fade over time. There's no way to stay besties with everyone you've ever met.

EMBRACE FRIENDSHIPS
WITH ANYONE

I love videos of unlikely animal friends. Monkeys being friends with dogs. Goats and cats snuggling together. Based on the number of Reddit threads devoted to these friendships, I think a lot of other people love them, too. These animals are friends because they didn't judge the other before deciding to go for it.

So why don't we do that?

When we were in elementary school, we were friends with everyone; mostly because we were surrounded by the same two dozen people all day and our developmental skills hadn't evolved enough to discern who we wanted to hang out with. Really, anyone who embraced the concept of sharing was good with us. If they had a spare Snack Pack, even better.

Once we get into middle school, hobbies and social circles tend to segregate us. By high school, our core group often looks and thinks very similarly to the way we do. We all "grew up" together so we all tend to share the same ideas. There's nothing fun in that. It's boring. You're all just saying things to which everyone responds, "Yeah, I totally agree," and the conversation stops there.

Remember the kid in class who was in band, the school play, on the soccer team, and class president? They could be friends with everyone because they fit in every circle. That can still be you.

It's simple. Be friends with anyone. It will cost you nothing to step outside your friendship comfort zone. Trust me, it's completely risk-free. You never know where your next close friendship is going to come from, but if you only hang out with the same people who have the same interests and the same beliefs as you, then where's the fun?

Wouldn't it be great if we could have a diverse circle of friends, all of whom were different enough to keep life interesting? I love having debates with friends on current events. Those debates are constantly perforated by laughter as opposed to social media debates which are stuck in the stale, suffocating vacuum of the Internet.

How would you rather grow as a person? Surrounded by friends with whom you feel comfortable talking about tough topics, or by reading about tough topics on the Internet?

Be the monkey and the dog. Get out there and make a friend. Go talk to someone you might not normally talk to. Who knows where it could lead.

Give It A Fucking Shot

- ☐ Talk to the person behind you in line at the grocery store; even if they're not someone you'd normally talk with.

- ☐ Go to an event you may not normally go to.

- ☐ If a friend invites you a party or social event you would otherwise you say no to, go and see if you meet someone interesting.

OVERCOME SOCIAL LABELS

I've always been a pretty outgoing person, even when I'm not writing the most intimate details of my life in a book for strangers to read. I'm the kind of person who's described as energetic, quirky, and positive. But I'm not always those things. Sometimes I'm calm, reserved, and introverted.

Society loves to label us as one or the other. You're either introverted or extroverted. Analytical or creative. Leader or follower. There's pressure for us to be defined by these labels and then to stick them, no matter what.

I'm an ambivert. I'm very extroverted with friends and people I'm comfortable with, in scenarios I feel confident in, and then when the time comes for me to relax and have some "me" time, I become rather introverted.

I'm not the kind of person who likes big events. If I'm invited to an event with a plus one, my initial reaction is, "Can my dog count as my plus one?"

I thought because I was considered outgoing or extroverted that I always had to be "on" and that I would be disappointing people if I wasn't. That's just not a sustainable way to live. No person can be super excited and confident all the time.

Once I started saying no to certain invitations and started taking more time for myself, I noticed how much I enjoyed my introvert time. It made my extroverted, social time so much more authentic because I didn't have to force a smile when I didn't want to. I could just relax into the moment and trust that whatever I was feeling was right. Now, I no longer judge myself based on who I'm "supposed to be" at any given moment.

Knowing it's okay be either introverted or extroverted at any given moment makes it easier for me to interact with others, to meet and connect with new friends, and to be honest with my friends and family. If I'm not feeling talkative like I normally might be and a family member says, "What's going on? Are you okay?", my answer can simply be, "Yep. I'm good, just having an introverted day."

I used to feel the need to qualify those moments with, "I've had a long week," or, "I'm pretty tired, I didn't sleep great last night," which half of the time wasn't even true. I needed an excuse and those sounded like ones that wouldn't evoke a follow up question. Really, I just wasn't feeling amped, and that's totally fine. I'm not a jumbotron in Times Square—I don't have to always be on.

I always appreciate when people check in with me, and still encourage my loved ones to do so if they feel something's off. I didn't want to change that aspect of my relationship with friends and family, but now my response is truthful instead of what I think they want to hear.

REDEFINE YOUR RELATIONSHIP WITH YOUR PARENTS

Remember the first time you cursed in front of your parents? Like, really cursed. In a casual conversation you slipped in a "fuck" and thought, "Wow, my relationship with my parents is so evolved now. I cursed." No? Okay. Maybe that was just me then.

Remember the first time you realized your parent was a person just like everyone else? That they had fears and emotions just like all people do? That they didn't have all the answers or could solve all the problems in the world? That they made mistakes, too? That moment is undeniable. It's the moment they stopped being omniscient to us.

Parents will always have a hard time seeing their little baby as a full-grown adult. They'll have trouble, at least for a while, letting you make your own choices and your own mistakes. You'll always have a parent/child relationship because let's be honest, they can't un-raise you. You can, however, redefine how your relationship looks and feels.

If your relationship with your parents by the time you reach adulthood is positive, then it's a matter of making sure they see you as an adult and respect you enough to have adult conversations. I'm still sometimes befuddled when I leave a conversation with my dad about the current political climate, or I talk to my mom about the problems she's having at work like I would any other friend. It's weirdly freeing to have this kind of dynamic with them because we've reached a level of honesty we never could have achieved when I was younger.

If your relationship is not so positive with your parent or parents—perhaps one was distant or absent during your childhood, or abusive or neglectful—it can be a different story. Whatever the toxicity was, you now get to heal from it. Healing from trauma can help you become the badass, strong person you were always meant to be. You get to set boundaries to aid in that healing, too. Part of being an adult is teaching others how you want to be treated, and that's no different for a parent, or any family member, than it would be with any other type of relationship.

It's okay to say:

- "I don't think it's healthy for us to talk this way anymore."
- "I don't think that's a good topic for us to discuss."
- "I need some space from you as I redefine our dynamic."
- "I no longer think this relationship is healthy for me."

There comes a moment when you realize your parents are just people. If it hasn't happened yet, just wait. It will. They (hopefully) did the best they could in raising you, but everyone messes up. No parent can raise a child perfectly or be a perfect parent all the time. Everyone has trauma from their childhood; it's inevitable. As adults, we get to make the choice of how we address that trauma, and part of that can be changing how we interact with our parents. The ball's not entirely in their court anymore.

You can have real, honest conversations with your parents and get some clarity on why they made the choices they made in raising you. They might shed a little light on their side of the curtain because let's be honest, we were center stage for most of our younger years. We were so wrapped up in our own kid world that we didn't really notice what our parents were up to. We barely saw what was happening behind the scenes.

Give It A Fucking Shot

- ☐ Talk with your parents about any questions you may have about your childhood.

- ☐ If you're working through some trauma from childhood, ask them questions or have honest conversations to help the healing process.

- ☐ Start by writing down some questions you might want to ask them.

- ☐ Set a time to talk with them.

REDEFINE YOUR RELATIONSHIP WITH YOUR SIBLINGS

My brother and I tortured each other in really specific ways when we were younger. If he pissed me off, I wouldn't yell or hit him, but I'd set his clock forward an hour so his alarm would go off an hour early, or I'd put a Jewel CD in his stereo so when his friends were over listening to music, they would think he loved Jewel. I told you—specific.

We were also really close growing up. He's about two and a half years younger than me, but we shared mutual friends, interests, and hobbies. Most of my friends hated their siblings, or at the very least fought with them a lot, but I thought my brother and I were cool. We were like kids on a sitcom who fought but then forgot what we were fighting about ten minutes later. We had each other's backs.

As we got older, we got to know each other as people. Much like redefining your relationship with your parents, sibling relationships also evolve. This one can be trickier, though, because you're now equals and in completely different competitions.

Let's back it up a second. When I was a kid, I was into volleyball, school plays, and hanging with my friends. My brother liked none of those things and was mostly obsessed with soccer, which I had little interest in. Our competitive natures were rarely directed at one another. I'm also the older sibling so I always felt like I had the upper hand. I knew words he didn't. I understood higher-level concepts than he did. Even when my brother was graduating high school, I wrote him a little guide on how to navigate college (not the classes but parties, roommates—the real shit. I guess that was the unofficial prequel to this book). I had always had the role of imparting knowledge on him. He always had the role of learning from me. It wasn't until we were full-fledged adults that competition became an element.

When I was in my mid-twenties, my brother graduated from college and got a job in the financial sector. He was now making more money than me, even though I was older, which, contrary to my objections with the universe, doesn't matter after a certain age. He bought a condo before I did. He traveled to countries I wanted to go to before I was able to get there first. Hell, he published papers before this book was even a thought in my head. He was passing me on certain milestones I thought had to be achieved in a certain linear order. No longer did it matter that I was born first. I couldn't solve grown-up problems setting an alarm clock one hour ahead. I had to own my own shit in this now.

So why did it matter if he did things before I did? I didn't care if friends or colleagues did things before I did. I was happy for him and his success. The real issue was that our dynamic was shifting. We were no longer in lockstep as two kids in a certain age bracket—we were now adults doing things our own way. We had become people with individual paths. We had to figure out how to navigate this, or rather, I did. I had to realize it wasn't a race to an imaginary finish line. With time, none of those things bothered me anymore because I could see him as his own person and recognize that he had value beyond the label of "my younger brother."

Now we're able to grab a beer and laugh about our personal failures, revel in each other's successes, and make fun of each other the way only siblings who have spent their whole lives together can.

BE OKAY WITH PEOPLE NOT LIKING YOU

Oh, this one is a constant struggle for me.

When I was in sixth grade, I came home crying from school one day. My mom asked me what was wrong, and I responded, "Lauren said she didn't like me." She looked at me, in only a way a caring mother could, and said, "It's okay if not everyone likes you. You don't like everyone you meet. That's okay."

While her response sounds like it would devastate me, it actually relieved me. I no longer had to be perfect. I no longer had to spend so much time and energy making everyone on this planet like me because sometimes, they just won't. All I had to do was be me. Phew. Load off my back.

Or so I thought. It turns out that, much like thinking I could pull off bangs, I had to learn this lesson over and over again throughout my life. It was fine to have a schoolmate not like me, but what do I do when a boy I have a crush on doesn't like me? Or when a boss doesn't like me and I'm up for a promotion?

You deal. That's what you do. Because most of the time, someone not liking you has absolutely nothing to do with you. We've heard it before. "You're not everyone's cup of tea." Of course you aren't. You don't like every flavor of tea or type of food, so why would you like every person? And why would they all, unanimously, like you? You're not Baby Yoda. Sure, you're awesome, but some people don't like your kind of awesome.

When I was younger, I tried to be sporty to fit in with the jock boys, and I tried to enjoy playing dress up to fit in with the girly girls, but neither of those things were really me. It was exhausting trying to be someone I wasn't just so people would like me.

No matter how hard you try to make everyone in the world love you, and you them, there are still some people out there that won't respond to you the way you want them to. That has nothing to do with you and is out of your control. The only person you can control is you. The people who gravitate towards your amazing, authentic self are your people.

If you're a people pleaser like me, do all you can to be kind and generous to others and then let the rest go. Be okay with someone not liking you because there are a million others who do.

PART THREE

MIND
SHIT

PUT YOURSELF OUT THERE

I know. Even the title of this section is scary. People can be annoying. Who wants to meet more of them?

I get it. But imagine this—you're settled down fifty years from now, looking back on your life and thinking about the concert you never went to, or the person you never dated because you were too scared to talk to them.

When you tell people to put themselves out there, the response usually sounds something like, "But what happens if it doesn't work out?", "What happens if it fails?", "What happens if they don't like me back?", "What happens if it doesn't go like I imagined it?"

Then you're exactly where you are right now, but with a story. You can either sit here and do nothing or you can put yourself out there, and if your effort fails, come right back to where you were. Even if it results in heartache, even if you stumble and fall, at least you did something. You got to feel something. Otherwise, you're living the exact same day 20,000 times. How boring is that?

Most likely, the fear you're experiencing is purely based in the unknown. You're not actually fearing meeting people but fearing how they'll react to you. You're not actually fearing a new activity, but instead fearing the possibility of failing at that activity.

That's perfectly normal. You're comfortable in the life you have, with the people you know, doing the things you like. But there's no room to flourish there. You're static. Something amazing could be just out of reach but you'll never know if you don't extend your hand and grab it.

SHIT ADULTS NEVER TAUGHT US

If you combine this advice with the previous chapters, you could form new friendships and even learn a skill for a future side hustle—all by doing one new thing. Why not take the risk and attempt something new? Don't let a fear of failure stop you from ever trying something. Because if you don't even try, I'm certain you won't succeed.

Give It A Fucking Shot

- ☐ Join a club.

- ☐ Take a class (cooking, photography, anything with others).

- ☐ Book a trip somewhere.

- ☐ Go on a date.

- ☐ Go dancing.

DO THINGS THAT SCARE YOU

This takes "putting yourself out there" one step further. Doing things that scare you may seem like a terrifying concept, but it's been proven that getting out of your comfort zone is one of the fastest ways to grow. There's clarity on the other side of fear.

Now, I want to be crystal clear—doing things that scare you does not mean walking down a dark alley alone at night yelling, "I have $800 in my wallet." There is a huge difference between doing things that scare you and doing things that are stupid.

When I was seventeen years old, I graduated from high school in the Maryland town I'd lived in since I was five. I had been accepted to several colleges, but chose the one farthest away in Orlando, Florida. I was so excited to go to college. I had even started packing my things three months before I left for school. The anticipation of a new adventure was almost too much to handle. When the time finally came, I drove the fourteen hours to Orlando, blinded by the excitement of being on my own for the first time in my life. I focused so hard on the activity of setting up my dorm and starting my classes that once I had finished settling in, fear snuck in and took over. I was alone for the first time in my life. I knew no one. I barely knew how to get around town (it was the pre-smartphone days). There was no turning back, I was already enrolled. So, I let the fear fuel my decisions. I started making friends with the other people in my dorm so I could alleviate the fear of not knowing anyone. I gravitated towards other out-of-state kids because we shared the common denominator of being new in town. I started taking little day trips with my new friends to get a feel for the town. Instead of being crippled by fear, I used it to inspire me to try new things.

On the other side of my fear was an incredible experience I wouldn't have had otherwise. If I had gone to a school near my hometown, with people I knew from high school, I might not have learned how to be so independent. I might not have gotten a taste for new cities and experiences that later stimulated my love of travel and adventure.

Fear isn't one side of a coin. It's one side of a die. If you roll, you'll find excitement, passion, joy, courage, and endless possibilities are all on the other sides.

If you've had a crush on someone for a year and never asked them out because it scares you— ask them out.

If you don't go to that spin class because you're afraid of looking stupid—go spin your ass off.

If you've wanted to try jet skiing or paddle boarding but don't because you're scared of falling off—go this weekend.

If you've wanted to go to Portugal for years but no friends are ever available to go with you—book the flight and go alone.

You'll be so thankful you did it when you're on the other side. Even if it doesn't go like you wanted it to, your mind will no longer be filled with "what ifs" and will instead be filled with amazing memories.

Who cares if the experience isn't exactly as you imagined it? It could be better. Or you could learn something just from stepping outside your cozy, safe space. If you finally ask out your crush and the date sucks, at least you know you can survive a bad date. You didn't die. Now go ask out someone else and give it another try.

If you went to Portugal and the touristy sights weren't as incredible as you had imagined, go back another time and see different things. Or go somewhere else on your next trip. Now you can explore a new place without the fear of being alone.

Each time you do something that scares you, it gets a little easier. That's how confidence is built. And damn it, confidence is sexy.

Give It A Fucking Shot

☐ Pick one thing that scares you and sign up for it. Don't think, just do it.

☐ If you're afraid to do it alone, ask a friend to join you. Maybe they've wanted to go on an adventure too but were also too scared.

"THE BEST THING YOU COULD DO IS MASTER THE CHAOS IN YOU. YOU ARE NOT THROWN INTO THE FIRE. YOU ARE THE FIRE."

— DEIDRA RAE

DON'T BE AFRAID TO START OVER

So, you went to four years of college, four years of graduate school, spent two years interning, finally landed your dream job... and you hate it.

That's okay. Would you rather be unhappy forever chasing a dream you once had, or be brave enough to start over today and be happy for the rest of your life doing something you're truly passionate about?

So what if you're forty years old and woke up one day thinking that you no longer want to have the career you have. Start over. Don't be afraid. It's a chance to start something better this time.

If you're forty years old and thinking of going back to school but don't want to because when you graduate, you'll be forty-four and you think that's too old to start a new career, I've got bad news for you. In four years, you'll still be forty-four, whether you went to school or not. At least you could be forty-four and doing something you love. You aren't starting over at forty-four; you're starting fresh.

When you start over, it's not like you're going back to the dugout waiting to be called up to bat. You're not even starting at the batter's box. You start on first base at the very least, because no one can ever take away the experiences you've had. So you worked in accounting for fifteen years and realized one day you want to open a restaurant. You aren't starting over—you have a great head for business and can predict problems others wouldn't be able to see coming. Your experience translates from one career to another, even when it isn't obvious how.

Maybe you had a summer job once that turned into a decade-long career. You're about to get promoted but you can't shake the feeling in your gut that you don't want it. It's okay to walk away from the money, the opportunity, the life you could've had. You're really only walking away from something that isn't right for you and walking towards something that is. If you don't change course now, you'll continue to grow unhappier and will probably change your career in a few years anyways. By then you'll be a few years older and a move might be even harder to make because new life stuff got in the way.

I was once told by a teacher that you'll never have more time or less responsibility than you do right now. That's right—this moment right now. You'll get busy, like we all do, with life. You'll take on more responsibilities (get promoted, start a family, add side projects, buy a house) and life will get more complicated, as it always seems to do. When people say, "There is no time like the present," they mean, you don't know what life holds after this moment, so if you can do it now, do it. You could be abducted by aliens tomorrow and be forever upset about all the things you never got to finish on Earth.

If there is a way to dabble in something new without completely leaving your current situation, do that. If you've always wanted to be a writer, filmmaker, or entrepreneur, start doing things on the side to confirm it's truly your passion before you make the leap. The *Consider A Side Hustle* chapter at the beginning of this book could help you get started. If you're afraid that starting something new might take up too much time, grab a partner. A friend might be wanting a change too, and between the two of you, you can split the workload and still grow something amazing together.

Think back on the past ten years—didn't they go by so fast? Sure, a lot of stuff happened during that time, but time flew, didn't it? Life isn't slowing down. Life isn't pumping the brakes so you can have a minute to think things over and make a change when the timing feels right. Life is always going to keep moving forward. Whether you make a change today or not, the next ten years are still going to happen. In ten years, when you look back on this moment right now, will you be wishing you made a change sooner? Change is scary. Regret is scarier. Don't let your life plan make you miserable.

ENJOY TIME ALONE

It took me a long time to get this one down. Whenever I was alone, I needed the TV on, or music playing in the background. Even in quiet, relaxing moments, I found myself scrolling through some random app on my phone for no reason other than I needed something to do. I wasn't okay just being.

I didn't eat alone in a restaurant until I was twenty-seven. I also traveled alone for the first time at twenty-seven. I saw my first theater show alone on that trip. I went to my first movie alone at twenty-eight. And guess what I figured out once I started doing stuff totally alone? I like me.

I don't need to wait for my friends' schedules to free up or for me to be dating someone to do something. This realization sparked my interest to travel out of the country alone, and that's where I really found that being alone is amazing.

When you travel alone, you aren't beholden to what anyone else wants to do. You have the space to think your own thoughts and formulate your own impressions of an experience. Most importantly, you'll find that experiences can be just as enjoyable by yourself as they can be with others.

Doing things alone gave me so much more confidence to stand on my own. In moments when I felt like an outsider—at parties where I didn't know anyone or when starting a new job—I knew that even if I found myself totally alone, I'd be okay.

If you aren't good at being alone, I challenge you to try it. Start small. Take yourself on a date. Go to a movie you've been wanting to see or to a restaurant you've been wanting to try. Go for a hike alone. Or take a drive for a few hours totally alone and explore a nearby town.

So many people stay in bad situations because of the fear of being alone. They jump from one relationship to another. They fill their weekends with hangouts while they burn themselves out from exhaustion. Finding that you enjoy your own company prevents you from making these mistakes.

It's going to feel weird at first. The first time I went to see an Off-Broadway show by myself, my seat was sandwiched between an adorable couple and a group of friends having the time of their lives. When I first sat down, I felt a rush of loneliness. Then the adorable couple started to bicker, and the group of friends were fighting over snacks they were passing back and forth. I felt content in the fact that I got to enjoy this experience for myself. I never had to worry about sharing snacks—they were all for me. No one was going to taint this experience with a petty argument because there was no one to bicker with. The experience was entirely in my control.

I find that the best way to ease into being comfortable alone is to start by doing things you know you love. If you love going out to eat, take yourself to a restaurant you've been dying to try. If you're a music lover, discover new local bands by taking yourself to a show. It'll check an activity off your wish list and your awkward feelings should be minimal because you're doing something you already know you love.

If dinner seems too intense, try lunch or grabbing a quick drink after work. Don't rush it. Let yourself sit in the discomfort, if any creeps in. You'll move past it, I promise you. You're just not used to being alone.

If that's too scary, practice going for a walk totally alone. No cell phone. No distractions. Just you, alone in the world. Do this for a few minutes each day and see how it feels.

Once you feel comfortable with the stuff you love, you can move on to the more adventurous stuff, like traveling alone or trying a new hobby.

The goal is to just enjoy you. You get to spend your whole life with you, so why not enjoy every minute?

Give It A Fucking Shot

- ☐ This month, take yourself on a you-date. Just you. No one else.

- ☐ If it goes well, try another next month.

- ☐ If it seemed too overwhelming, try something smaller next month and work your way back up.

CALM ANXIETY

Let me just start by saying if anxiety burned calories, I'd never have to exercise a day in my life. While anxiety for me has always ebbed and flowed like the tide, it seems to remain, in one way or another, a constant. It may not be noticeable all the time, but like a fart during a yoga class, anxiety always finds the least convenient moments to present itself.

We all get anxious. Anxiety comes in short spurts and longer, more prolonged episodes. If you have a more prolonged form of anxiety that lasts over two or three weeks, consider seeking help. A therapist could be a great place to start.

The sudden, short-lasting spurts of anxiety are the ones I'm well-versed in. Sometimes my anxiety feels like a rollercoaster of unwelcome emotions and I can't seem to get off the ride. Sometimes it's like a worry-inducing movie trailer of my future that gets stuck playing on repeat in my head. Sometimes it feels like an unexpected heat wave in the middle of winter. Not all anxiety presents the same way. However, when the unwelcome guest of anxiety shows up for you, here are some tricks to send it packing.

THE TONGUE TRICK
Where is your tongue right now? Is it on the roof of your mouth? Loosen your jaw and let your tongue fall from the roof of your mouth. Take a few deep breaths, in through your nose and out through your mouth.

THE 3-3-5 TRICK

I like to do this one before job interviews or functions where I know I'll need to be calm but can't seem to get there. Sit comfortably for a moment, close your eyes, and take a deep breath into your belly for three seconds. Now hold the breath for three seconds. Next, let it out slowly for five seconds. Repeat this for a minute or two until you feel a better sense of calm.

EMOTIONAL POWER RELEASE TRICK

Close your eyes and check in with your soul. Take a deep breath and put a name to the emotion you are feeling right now. As you exhale, whisper the emotion, whether it's "overwhelmed," "worry," "fear," or "anger." Naming your emotions removes their power.

THE BODY CLENCH TRICK

Tense up all of the muscles in your body. Do it, right now, like you're about to turn into The Hulk. Now release each muscle one by one. First your feet, then your ankles, then your calves, then your knees, then your thighs, all the way up to your shoulders, then your neck, and lastly, your head (tongue, eyes, ears).

MINI GROUNDING TRICK

Close your eyes (in a safe, comfortable space). Now listen. What's the farthest noise you hear? Are you sure? Try listening for something farther than that. Is it a bird in the distance? Is it the wind, and if so, how far is the wind? Is it a car driving in the opposite direction? Now try listening for something even farther.

Once you find the farthest sound, focus on that for a moment.

Now, what's the closest noise you hear? Is it a person nearby? Is it a door closing in the other room? Is it the air-conditioning above you? Is it your own breath? Is it the hairs in your nose when you breathe? Focus on that sound for a moment.

Now open your eyes and focus for a moment on the first thing you see. Breathe into the calm of the noises around you while focusing your eyes on one spot. Stare at this spot and focus on your breathing.

If you don't feel calm yet, try this again in a minute or two.

MAJOR GROUNDING TRICK
This one is similar to the method above, but you'll do it with your eyes open using a more structured list.
Look around and identify the following:

> 5 things you can see
> 4 things you can feel
> 3 things you can hear
> 2 things you can smell
> 1 thing you can taste

Try to be aware of your breath as you noticing these things. The point is to focus less on your anxiety, get out of your head, and focus on the things around you. It doesn't matter if you pick the five "right" or "best" things you can see, just pick five things. Don't judge the process.

THE RAIN TRICK
I have a Spotify playlist of just rain. It's about two hours of rain tracks. They vary in length and type (some are gentle patters, some are thunderstorms), but in moments when I need to find calm, I pick one and put in on repeat, or let the playlist play through.

GUIDED MEDITATION TRICK
There are a ton of short and long meditations on YouTube or even various phone apps. Try to save a few of these for the moments when you need one. You can make a YouTube playlist or subscribe to certain channels so in moments of anxiety, they're easy to find. The last thing you need to be doing when you're stressed is looking for a meditation.

BELIEVE EVERYONE DESERVES HELP

I was having a conversation with a close friend from childhood when he said the most heartbreaking thing to me. We were discussing Anthony Bourdain, the incredibly talented chef and world-traveling documentarian who took his own life in the summer of 2018. In this discussion my friend said to me, "He was amazing. He really deserved help."

I was taken aback. First, yes. He did deserve help, but so does everyone. The fact that my friend, who has struggled on and off with depression himself, thought that because Bourdain was famous and brought entertainment to people, he "deserved" mental health treatment and interventions more than non-famous people was disheartening.

For the record, in case there was any doubt, everyone deserves help. Everyone. End of story.

There isn't a club of people who deserve better treatment because of their very specific specialty or contribution to society. If you are struggling with feelings of depression, anxiety, hopelessness, or anything you're genuinely unsure how to navigate on your own, get help. Anxiety and Depression Association of America, and Substance Abuse and Mental Health Services Administration are great places to start.

You deserve help for the person you are right now. Not the person you used to be. Not the person you could be. The person who is reading this sentence at this moment.

Just like it doesn't matter who you are, it also doesn't matter how depression looks in you. Depression doesn't look the same in everyone. Just because the guy who sat next to you in chemistry mentioned he has depression and you don't share any of his depressive traits doesn't mean you don't also have some form of depression. There are many different manifestations of depression and anxiety disorders. Chemistry dude may have insomnia and feel restless while you're exhausted and uninterested in normal life.

According to Mental Health America, out of all the people suffering from severe depression, only one-third of them will seek professional help. This includes therapy, medications and other forms of treatment. Why do so few people seek help when it comes to mental health?

I feel like society took a hard pendulum swing on the stance of mental health. A few decades ago, we never mentioned mental health disorders, like depression, because there was a major stigma around them. Now, people use depression as a feeling to describe their emotions about normal things in everyday life rather than a disorder.

"I can't believe 'Breaking Bad' is over. I'm so depressed." No, you're not. You're sad.

So, let's break down the difference. Depression is a diagnosable disorder stemming from a chemical imbalance in your brain. Sadness is a feeling based on current circumstances.

Think back to one of your first-ever geometry lessons in school: a square is a rectangle, but not all rectangles are squares. Depression is sadness but not all sadness is depression.

If you're having feelings of sadness but you know in your heart they'll pass eventually, if you're still able to go about all your normal activities, if you're still looking forward to plans down the road and hanging out with friends, chances are you're experiencing sadness. It can be debilitating at times but is usually based on a current situation.

If you're feeling very secluded, like the sadness you're experiencing is a never-ending downward spiral and nothing present or future matters, please put down this book and seek help. You deserve it. Don't be one of the two-thirds of people who ignore these symptoms assuming they'll go away on their own.

Someone today is having the best day ever—right now. As you're reading this, there are people in the world living moments that will change their lives forever. The love of their life said, "I love you" for the first time, their first child was born after years of trying to conceive, the company they built from the ground up made its first sale. If those people had given up, they never would have made it to this moment. Keep going—your moments are coming. If you need help to get there, just ask. You deserve help just like you deserve all the amazing moments to come.

Okay, I'm done with the mid-book PSA. You may now resume your regularly scheduled reading.

REALIZE GUILT AND REGRET
ARE USELESS EMOTIONS

Okay, fine. Guilt and regret are not *entirely* useless. They are, however, entirely about you. They're emotions that prevent you from moving forward, from forgiving yourself and finding peace. Unlike most other downward-spiraling emotions like sadness, frustration, and anger; guilt and regret don't want you to work through them. Instead, they paralyze you in a quicksand of shame.

Everyone's done things they wish they hadn't. I can think back on some embarrassing thing I did ten years ago and cringe just picturing it. But there's nothing I can do to change the past. I can't un-wear platform boots with gray Limited Too sweatpants to school in tenth grade, so why regret that outfit choice? It's causing me shame over a decade later, but it's affecting no one else's life.

I also can't un-hurt my friend's feelings in college when I didn't invite her out dancing with our group. I can own it, learn from it, apologize for it, but regretting it doesn't help either of us.

We all know that when these things happen, we should apologize in the sincerest way and hope the person we hurt forgives us. Just know that if you've apologized and done all you can to make amends, that's all you can do. There's no purpose in carrying the guilt and regret of past decisions around with you. You're only hurting yourself. Guilt and regret will never change the past, but they will affect your future if you let them.

Quick reminder: We're all just human. Our lives are made up of a series of moments of profound humanity. Humanity isn't all joy and bliss. It's filled with sadness, and anger, and frustration, and love, and humility, and compassion, and hope, and so many other wonderful and devastating emotions. But there are a few moments that stop us from feeling all that it means to be human and those are encapsulated in the shame bubble. Those are the moments that paralyze us in feelings so deep that they prevent us from moving on.

My regret and guilt like to show up to the party in different outfits. One of their favorites is "not my fault." I've had my fair share of car accidents in my life. Thankfully, no one has ever been majorly injured, but my instinct after each accident has always been that it's "not my fault." It's the other car's fault, the traffic light's fault, the icy road's fault, the trash truck's fault (true story—I hit a trash truck). Blaming things outside myself for my mistakes is just my guilt and regret trying to deflect responsibility off me and onto something else.

If you failed at something and you regret doing it, that's okay. You'll probably fail again at some point. If you hurt someone and you feel guilty about how you treated that person, that's okay. Apologize and learn from it. We are a string of mistakes put together to form a life. If we don't make mistakes and learn from them, we don't grow. If we make the same mistakes over and over again, we're no longer making mistakes—we're forming habits. Don't regret it, change it.

If you loved and got your heart broken, don't regret the relationship. Grow from it. Find someone who won't hurt you that way and learn your own value from that experience. If you loved and broke someone else's heart, don't guilt-trip yourself forever. Grow from that, too.

If you said something to a friend that hurt their feelings, let them know you fucked up and ask them how you can fix it.

I don't know you. But I know you regret the hurt you've caused people. I know you feel guilty about the bad choices you've made. I forgive you. So, go forgive yourself.

You don't have to carry around your mistakes forever. That's like carrying around a backpack of expired groceries. It's heavy. Put it down. Keep walking with the knowledge you gained from the experience, but don't carry with you the full weight of your mistakes. You'll only walk slower.

ACCEPT THAT LOSSES DEMAND GRIEF

Grief comes in as many shades as the rainbow. Like a bright, neon yellow, there's the in-your-face kind of grief, namely someone passing away. It's an undeniable grief because this person is no longer physically in your life. Then there are the more subtle, muted shades of grief. The jasmine, sandy, tan forms, if you will. A relationship ends. A job is lost. A beloved item goes missing. Something that's important to you is gone. The thing is, it doesn't matter what shade it comes in; grief demands to be felt.

When something is taken from your life, it shakes your foundation. The things you counted on to be in your life are no longer certain to be there forever. The comfort you previously had in this piece of your life is now gone and you're forced to sit in the discomfort while you adjust your life to fit your new reality. It's super unfair and confusing. How's a person supposed to deal with something like that?

You work through it. You've probably heard that the five stages of grief are:

- Denial
- Anger
- Bargaining
- Depression
- Acceptance

You know that easy to remember acronym, DABDA? No? Don't

worry; it's not vital you know these stages by heart. Just be aware that they exist as you move through them.

They don't always come in that order, or any order, and they can happen all at once, two or three at a time, or swing back and forth. These five stages are just emotions you will likely feel at some point during the grieving process. Simply put, just because you've accepted something doesn't mean it won't still hurt when you think about it later. It won't mean that in five years, a memory won't cause anger or sadness. Grief comes and goes. There's no timetable. You can't control it, no matter how much you want to.

A year after my nine-year relationship ended, I was watching a movie and a scene made me think of my ex and I started to cry. I talked to my therapist the next day and said, "It was so stupid. It's been a year. I've moved on. I'm in such a good place. Why haven't these moments stopped?" All she said was, "Why do you think a year later it should be any different?"

Why did I think it should be different? Because people on the Internet made me think that if I'd moved on, I'd never look back? Because I'd read a story of a woman whose husband of forty years died and who got remarried two years later? I realized the only reason I thought I should be somewhere else was because I made a TON of assumptions about what this form of grief would look like with very little evidence. The only evidence I should have, or could have, is me. How I work through things, how I process these moments. And even that isn't enough, because each situation is different. There was no way to Google my way out of grief.

I'd felt grief when a friend of mine died when I was in college. I'd felt grief when my best friend in elementary school moved away and went to a different middle school.

Hell, I was sad for a week when my favorite TV show ended. I took a weekend to emotionally recover when a job I loved ended.

Loss doesn't always come from someone dying. It's very painful when someone exits our lives in some way but still wanders the earth just as they had before they entered it. It can ache when something in our lives that we held dear, that made us feel safe, is now no longer there.

So, let me be one to say that when a relationship ends, it's okay to grieve. When a friend moves away, it's okay to grieve. When a chapter in your life ends, no matter how big or how small it is, it's okay to grieve.

"DON'T WALK TEN MILES INTO A FOREST AND EXPECT TO GET OUT IN FIVE."

— HARRY THE THERAPIST

UNDERSTAND THE ONLY WAY OUT IS THROUGH

Robert Frost once said, "The only way out is through." I had a teacher quote that to me one time and it inspired quite the visual. You can't go around something, only through it. I picture myself trying to find my way around a forest from inside of it. Like a giant hand reaches down, picks me up and carries me to the surface road just beyond the trees. But there is no giant hand in life. If I'm stuck inside of a forest, the only way out is to walk the fuck out.

What the phrase really means is, "You can't talk your way out of feelings." I've always been the type of person who hates feeling sad, angry, frustrated, or anything unpleasant. I use logic to talk myself out of it. I'll say to myself, "I shouldn't be mad at this situation, that's just life. Sometimes shitty things happen," as if I'm trying to talk myself out of being mad. Instead of just sitting in the anger, I'll use logic to say, "It's stupid to be mad at this so don't be, cool?"

With breakups, I have an immutable habit of distracting myself with work, friends, shopping—whatever helps to get my mind off of it. What I'm actually doing is making sure I'm busy enough that I don't have to feel anything. Then a few months go by and a commercial will come on that reminds me of that person and I'll burst into tears. I'll think, "What the hell? I'm over this." I'm not over it. I never even dealt with it. I just went around it, not through it.

In 2017, I ended a rather long relationship. I closed the bank accounts, he moved out, I got new furniture. Hell, I had even split the vet account to reflect he now had one dog and I had the other.

We were totally and completely separate now. We hardly spoke. I had moved on. On paper. About two months after our separation, I found myself really sad one weekend. I couldn't figure out why. I had finally stopped doing things to avoid feeling sad, so my body decided, "Ugh, finally. She's ready to feel some shit."

I've spent so much of my life trying not to feel shitty feelings—anger, sadness, frustration, betrayal, unworthy, unwelcome. When those feelings enter my body, it's like I've been submerged underwater. I'll do anything I can to come up for air. Each distraction is a breath. Every deflection of "I'm fine" is me bobbing my head above water. The late-night TV binge is me avoiding time with my thoughts. The drinks out with friends—even though I'm already exhausted—is me hiding from what's below the surface. But these moments don't get me anywhere. I'm not actually learning to deal with anything if I'm not acknowledging something needs dealing with in the first place. I'm just treading water. If I want to make it through something, I have to swim.

I love to skirt around anything that makes me sad or causes me anxiety. For me, those issues then come out in my body. If I've been having a lot of anxiety that I just keep pushing further and further down, I'll start getting migraines, or my skin will start to get hives. It's my body telling me I have to work through whatever I'm avoiding. I can't squish it down or ignore it anymore. I have to let it out.

So how do you let it out? You feel it. When you start to cry, don't judge it, don't stop it—just cry. When you have a few days of being sad, stop trying to distract yourself or fake being happy and just let yourself be sad for a few days.

Go through it, not around it. You'll feel better once you're out of the forest.

TRUST THAT TIME HEALS ALL

I had a friend who was put on an antibiotic for the first time at the age of twenty-five. She had a stubborn sinus infection that wasn't going away on its own and her doctor prescribed her Amoxicillin. Unfortunately, I'd been plagued with many similar infections in my life and was no stranger to antibiotics.

When we were out at dinner, she told me, "I don't think the antibiotics are working." I asked her how long she'd been on them to which she responded, "I took the first one this afternoon at like 2:00 but I don't feel any better yet."

I had to inform her that antibiotics don't work like Advil. You can't take it and expect to feel better within the hour. She was going to have to take them for the next ten days to really get rid of her infection. She thought she would start taking the pills and feel immediately better. "That's not how healing works," I said. You can put a bandage over a cut, but the scab will still be there for a while. You can pop an Advil for a sore throat, but not until the inflammation goes down will you be better.

The same is true for all wounds, even the ones we can't see. You can't just decide one day that you're better. Real healing takes time.

When I first started therapy in 2014, I told my therapist I'd only need a few sessions. I just had this one issue I wanted to work through, so I'd be all healed up and on my way in a few short weeks. Oh, how naïve I was. It was disappointing when I learned I couldn't heal years of built-up problems, anxiety, and interwoven personal flaws in a few weeks.

If you've gone through something traumatic, for example, there is no magic pill you can take to suddenly heal yourself from that trauma. You have to work through it, and some of that work is just letting time go by. Let the past get further in the rearview mirror and focus on the road ahead of you.

It can be incredibly aggravating that there's no way to speed up time. There's no special time machine that can transport you five years down the road, when everything is a distant memory. Even if there was, I doubt you'd want it. You'd be robbing yourself of growth, of becoming a stronger person, and of proving to yourself that you're a damn fighter. It may feel like time has stopped or that things won't improve but I promise you, they will. Time keeps moving forward and so will you.

In the meantime, just breathe and trust in time's power to heal all things.

CURB CATASTROPHIC THINKING

Sure, the word "catastrophic" seems a bit dramatic, but that's because it is. Catastrophic thinking is when your mind overreacts like a teenage drama queen and decides the worst-case scenario is the one that's going to happen, typically with little to no evidence.

Here are some examples:

> "I've had such a bad headache all day. It's probably a brain tumor. Oh shit, I'm dying now."

> "My boss just went into her office with the CEO and closed the door. They know I can hear them if the door's open. They're definitely talking about me. What did I do wrong? Oh my god. I'm about to get fired."

> "Shit. I'm stuck in traffic. I'm going to be five minutes late to this interview. They're definitely going to hate me. I'm not going to get the job. Why am I even going now? I'll never get the job I want anyways. My career is going nowhere."

> "I have a huge zit on my face. I can't go on this date. They're going to think I'm hideous. I don't know

why on earth I thought I was attractive enough to even go out with this person."

"I can't tell my girlfriend I hate that she leaves her dirty dishes everywhere. It's going to cause a fight and then she'll leave me. I'll never find anyone to love me if she leaves."

"I've been sad for so long now. I'm probably going to be depressed forever. I'll never be happy again. I'll just die like this."

Catastrophic thinking is like going down a log flume ride. It starts out calm and normal with a slow ascension. You're in a boat floating along, and then out of nowhere you're thrown down a deep slope and emerge soaking wet. It all seemed to be going fine before the nosedive into a turbulent landing. How did one innocent enough thought turn into a full-blown panic inducing thought process?

Well, you let yourself get swept up in the worst-case scenario and became so blinded by things going horribly wrong that you failed to notice the small probability of those things actually happening. Don't fret. There are things you can do.

Sure, there are medications and doctors out there designed to specifically help treat the underlying causes of severe catastrophic thinking, such as depression and anxiety. If you're more of a mild to moderate catastrophic thinker, try some of the steps below first, based loosely on the teachings of Dr. Karen Reivich, a University of Pennsylvania professor.

STEP 1
If you feel this type of thinking coming on, and you're able to recognize it, stop and talk to your brain. Say something like, "Hey. Knock it off. I know what you're doing up there. You're trying to make up shitty scenarios to stir up a little drama. Not cool."

STEP 2

Recognize that your brain's just being nuts and the probability of those scenarios actually happening is pretty small. Argue against your brain and try to convince yourself that everything's going to be fine. Prove your brain wrong. "The CEO isn't going to fire me because I've done an amazing job recently and I've done nothing worth firing me over." "I don't have a brain tumor because it's just a headache, I've had them before and they go away. I haven't even seen a doctor yet." "My girlfriend won't leave me if I point out she leaves dirty dishes everywhere. In fact, it will make us stronger because we will work through something together."

STEP 3

Okay, yes—there is a sliver of a chance you aren't nuts. Sure, the probability of the worst scenario coming true is very small but why not plan for it if it will calm your anxiety and make your brain shut the fuck up. Don't just make a plan. Believe in your plan. "If I show up to this job interview five minutes late and they're mad, I'll apologize and follow up later to show my dedication to the position." "If my date notices my zit, I'll laugh it off as stress or nerves and not let it affect the amazing time I'm going to have tonight."

STEP 4

Write down three ways you see this scenario going and how you would respond to each one. Pick one positive, one neutral, and one negative outcome.

1. My boss and the CEO closed the door because they're talking about a raise for me and life is about to be awesome.
2. They closed the door to discuss something that has nothing to do with me and life is going to remain the same, which is still awesome.
3. I'm getting laid off and will have to find a new

job. Less awesome, but I'll be totally fine if that happens.

Now create a positive spin on each of them.

1. If I get a raise or promotion, I'll do my best at the new job and prove to them they've made the right decision.
2. If this has nothing to do with me, then I'll go to lunch and enjoy the rest of my day.
3. If I get laid off, I'll have the opportunity to start at a new company, which might even mean more money or a promotion. I could even try a different field if I want.

Looking at that piece of paper will help you realize that you'll be okay with any of these outcomes. You'll survive no matter what. Most of the things you're likely worrying about won't even happen.

All of these steps help you build resilience. You're strong AF. Don't let catastrophic thinking make you doubt that.

ASK YOURSELF, IS THAT PROBLEM REAL?

This question seems to roll around in my head constantly: "Is that problem real?" More accurately it rolls around in my head as, "*Is that problem REAL?*" How many times a day is a problem I'm facing an actual, real problem?

Let me give you some small-scale examples.

> "I'm out of onion. Now I'll have to make something else for dinner."

> "It's raining. Now I have to change shoes."

> "There's traffic. Now I'll get home ten minutes late."

Small yet obvious, right? So what? I can eat other foods, wear other shoes, and start my TV show ten minutes later. Nothing bad actually happened; I just decided there was a problem because my brain felt like it. Now I'm moody for seemingly no reason.

I find that on days when I think like this, one of two things are true.

1. Everything feels like it has gone wrong.
2. Nothing feels like it has gone wrong.

If everything feels like it's gone wrong, then I'm looking for more problems to prove to myself that today sucks. Please, as if I don't already know that. If nothing's wrong and everything has been amazing for a week straight, somewhere in my brain I think it's too good to be true and I start looking for the flaw.

Let's look at some big-scale examples.

"My job is great, but I've been so bored since Tuesday. If I'm bored why am I staying? I should leave."

"My boyfriend and I haven't fought in months. I bet he's hiding something."

"My job, relationship, everything is going well. I need a change. What should I change?"

In all honesty, these thoughts aren't usually conscious. I'm never fully aware I'm having them, but they manifest in my actions. I start snooping around for a problem that doesn't exist and in the absence of one, I invent one. Remember catastrophic thinking? That's present here, too.

If it's been a few days of boredom, a few months of no fights, and things are going great, why blow up your life? Because when things get good, we get suspicious. Sometimes we feel a need to maintain some drama, so we ground ourselves in the worst way.

I've been in fights with people where they say, "Why are you in a mood right now?" to which I reply, "I really don't know." The real answer is that my brain believed things were either too shitty already or too good to be true, and I started inventing problems to confirm one of those beliefs.

Get in the habit of asking yourself the question, "Is this problem real?" It might be. The problem might actually be something that needs your attention and a well-constructed solution. It might also be a result of your brain getting bored and deciding to invent something out of nothing. Recognizing the difference could stop you from feeling like the whole world is out to get you.

STOP OVERTHINKING

I might as well have called this chapter, "Stop Overthinking, Natasha," since this is by far one of my worst qualities. It's how my anxiety often chooses to present itself. I have the horrible ability to see every outcome, no matter how plausible, for any scenario.

Do you ever go through the TSA security checkpoint at the airport and suddenly start freaking out thinking, "Shit, do I accidentally have a bomb in my bag?" I have. I've never touched a bomb. There's literally zero chance there is a bomb in my bag but my brain over thinks just for the hell of it to freak me out. If that sounds familiar, welcome to The Overthinkers Club. Your membership gift basket includes a "What If" bumper sticker and endless worry over mundane situations.

If someone makes me upset or frustrated, I'll spend hours awake in the middle of the night having conversations in my head with that person, figuring out the perfect thing to say.

If there's a possibility a problem may arise at a job (but is nowhere near becoming a reality), I'll think of five solutions for it, stressing over each detail.

If my partner says something to me, I'll analyze what they mean until I'm sure I've figured it out, often creating problems that weren't even there in the first place.

If a friend texts me something vague, I'll try to dissect their tone to see if they are mad or not.

If I'm booking travel, I'll plan for every possible scenario of what could go wrong.

Some people see this as a strength—to be as prepared as possible for any situation—but really, it's a form of anxiety. My overthinking stems from a feeling of control, or rather, a lack of control. If I can think of everything, then everything feels more controllable. I dissect all the possibilities to tame any potential chaos before it's even begun.

Here are some tools I've used to try and stop overthinking.

CATCH YOURSELF

When I enter the familiar pattern of overthinking, I try to catch myself. I'll say to myself, "There I go again. This isn't even real yet and I'm already overthinking it," or, "Why am I having a fight with a person in my head? They aren't even here. Just calm down and trust that this will work itself out."

REACH INTO THE ANXIETY ZONE

If I'm overthinking, chances are I'm anxious about something. It may not even be related to the topic steering my thought train, but there's anxiety setting up camp somewhere in my body and I've got to go hunt for it. Once I find and address the actual anxious problem, the overthinking tends to subside.

TALK IT OUT

Stuck in a spiral? Practicing fights in the shower against invisible people (which you always win, of course)? Try talking about it with a real person out loud. Even if it's not the person you're fake fighting with, try talking with a friend to see if this thought process is even worth exploring or if you start thinking, "Holy shit, I sound crazy," as the words come out of your mouth.

If none of this quite works to quiet that brain of yours, try the tricks from the *Calm Anxiety* chapter to calm your brain's over-activity.

Now stop overthinking about overthinking and move on to the next chapter.

FIND HAPPINESS NOW, NOT IN THE NEXT THING

One day around the time I first moved out on my own, I was driving in my beat-up Saturn SL2, trying to make my way through traffic. I kept thinking, "If I get a job where I can make enough to get a new car, my life will be great." About a year later, my Saturn crapped out on the side of the highway and I did get a new car, one I loved. But it didn't make my whole life instantly great.

Then one day a year or so later, I was sitting in the lobby of a production company, staring up at a beautiful chandelier while I waited to be interviewed for my dream job. I thought, "If I get this job, everything else will fall into place." And I got the job. But it didn't make everything fall into place.

For almost a decade, no matter how many people said, "Money can't buy happiness," or "Happiness is an inside job," it didn't resonate. I heard them. I just thought they were wrong. How could I not be happy if I had the dream home, the dream job, the dream car, the dream life? Barbie was happy with her dream house.

Apparently getting all the things you want only makes you happy if you're plastic. For humans, we have to learn that happiness isn't found in the next thing. Once you make a million dollars a year, your life will adjust to it in a flash and suddenly you'll think you need two million dollars a year to be truly happy. Then a hundred million. Then a billion. Money can't buy happiness because you'll always adjust your life to the money you have and there will always be something out of reach.

The method of finding happiness in the next thing doesn't work because nothing ever feels like we think it will. Getting that job, that partner, that house, never feels as good as we had hoped. You need to have dreams that are out of reach because that's what makes life worth living. If you had everything you wanted, then you'd be done and there wouldn't be anything to look forward to.

We're constantly setting ourselves up for disappointment when we believe that every situation we've created in our own minds will bring us happiness, rather than appreciating what's already in front of us. Imagining what could be limits our happiness with what we already have.

There's a method of practicing gratitude that helped me find happiness in the little things I already have. Every night before bed, I write down five things I'm grateful for.

When I started this practice, the first few nights were easy. I'm grateful for a comfortable house to live in. I'm grateful for a supportive family. Loving friends. Blah blah blah. Eventually, I started challenging myself not to repeat any of the things I was grateful for. I had to really think about it. My lists became less vague and way more random and specific. I'm grateful there was no line at the grocery store today. I'm grateful that my dog didn't bark while I was on an important phone call. I'm grateful that my favorite brand of jeans went on sale. I'm grateful my avocados didn't go bad before I remembered to eat them.

Once I had made it a habit of writing down what I was grateful for every night, I realized I was actually looking for things to be grateful for during the day. Something great would happen and I'd think, "Oh, awesome—that's definitely going in my gratitude journal tonight." Before I knew it, I started to feel happier and the people in my life started noticing. A coworker even asked me what was different. When I said, "Nothing," she said, "Huh. You seem lighter for some reason."

Nothing was different, except me. I stopped waiting to be happy. I stopped sabotaging my own happiness thinking I *had* to wait for it—that I couldn't be happy until the next chapter began.

There is no next chapter for happiness. You're not a Greek tragedy. You're a biography. Don't wait for page 200 to start enjoying your story.

TRUST YOU'RE CAPABLE
OF CHANGE

I don't pretend to be great at change. I'm fairly good at adapting to changes beyond my control but I'm definitely not great at initiating change. I've been in jobs longer than I should have. I've stayed in relationships longer than I should have. I've committed to brands of face wash long after I've decided they're basically just overpriced soap. Most of that had to do with my fear of change. I've spent a lot of time fearing the unknown, and as a result, remaining unhappy.

I'm capable of change. You're capable of change. Everyone is. The hard part is making sure it's the right change and then getting the courage to go for it.

Have you ever felt like you needed to change something in your life, and then changed one small thing and didn't feel any different? I've definitely done that. I've been accused of redecorating for no reason more than once. I would feel like things were stale, so I'd redesign a room—paint the walls, pack it with new furniture, hang new artwork. Then when it was all done, I'd feel completely the same. Satisfied in my work, but no different.

It's because I didn't change what I needed to. I was still too scared to change the things in my life that were bothering me so instead I'd change something that felt safe and inconsequential.

If you've been thinking about moving for a long time, maybe to another state, but haven't done it, moving two streets over won't satisfy that need. You first have to examine why you haven't made the leap to move. You can't cop out and say, "I don't like change," or, "I'm not very good at making decisions." That's bullshit. Sure, I've said those things before too, but they were bullshit when I said them. Use your emotional digging tools—*what's below that?*

You're completely capable of change. You're just scared of it. You're scared of not knowing what's on the other side of a decision, so you don't move forward with it. You're letting a chance of getting hurt stop you. You're letting a fear of the unknown stop you. You're probably letting a fear of failure stop you. You might even be letting a fear of success stop you.

Yeah, you read that last one right. Fear of success is a huge reason people don't change. When people get offered an interview at their dream company for the job they've been thinking about for ten years, do you know how many *don't* take it? A lot. They're scared that they may finally get what they want and be let down, or worse—let others down. They're scared the job won't be as good as they had imagined, or that they'll let the company down by not being absolutely, unattainably perfect. They sabotage themselves.

I've seen so many friends do this. They get a job interview and talk themselves out of it.

"I'm not sure I'll interview. I don't even know if that's what I want to do." Yes, you do. If you didn't know you wouldn't be thinking about it—you would have turned it down the second you got the interview. If you're thinking about it, go. Then decide once you have more information.

I've even seen this happen with people I've interviewed, too. I've reached out to seemingly perfect candidates and brought them in for interviews, and they've said things to me like, "I don't think I'm the right person for this." I've reviewed your resume and I know this company inside and out—why would I invite you in if I didn't think you were the right person? I'm trying to fill a position—why would I waste my time and yours if I didn't think you were right for it? That's just your self-esteem trying to talk you out of change because of the fear you won't be good enough.

We all have imposter syndrome sometimes. You get hired to do something you're definitely qualified for and think, "Oh shit. I'm going to let them down. They must think I'm better at this than I am." All you're doing is letting fear talk you out of something. You're probably going to be great at it.

Don't let fear stop you from taking a leap. If it doesn't work out like you imagined it would, you'll just change again. You are more than capable.

BREAK DOWN THINGS THAT OVERWHELM YOU

I overbook myself constantly. I'm a total people pleaser and if someone wants me to help them move, drive them to the airport, or help with a project, I'm there. I'll even work three jobs because I like to prove to myself that I can do anything.

Inevitably, I get overwhelmed by my constant need to take on more than I can handle, cramming tasks into an already busy week—like writing a book in between producing three commercials and helping out a friend with their film project.

I've found that when things get overwhelming, it's best to break them down.

Let's say that you have a long workday on Monday, dinner Monday night, a doctor's appointment Tuesday morning, a big meeting Tuesday afternoon, and a date Tuesday night.

That's a lot. Break it down, budget your time, and visualize your schedule in small sections. Here's an example.

MONDAY

9:00 a.m. – 7:00 p.m.	Work
7:05 p.m.	Leave for dinner
7:30 p.m. – 10:00 p.m.	Dinner
10:00 p.m.	Shower and then bed

Notes before bed:	Pick out date outfit and pack it in the car to change into tomorrow night

TUESDAY

8:00 a.m. – 9:00 a.m.	Doctor's appointment
11:00 a.m.	Prep for the meeting
12:00 p.m. – 1:00 p.m.	Big meeting
7:00 p.m.	Leave work for the date

Once you've broken it down, you'll see that everything can fit. If it still seems like too much, focus on one day at a time.

This works for tasks, too.

Have you ever had something that just sits on your to-do list year after year, hoping one day you'll find the energy to tackle it? Have you made the same New Year's resolution every January for the past decade?

Of course you haven't done it. It's too big. You can't just say to yourself, "Lose weight." That's not actionable.

But what if you broke down losing weight like this.

JANUARY: Join a gym and go eight times in January
JANUARY: Cut out soda

FEBRUARY: Increase gym visits to ten times this month
FEBRUARY: Cut out candy in addition to soda

MARCH: Go to the gym twelve times this month
MARCH: Cut out milk chocolate in addition to candy and soda

And so on and so on until voila, it's December and you actually tackled your goal.

What about finding a job? That's huge. Like, may-end-up-shaping-your-career-and-many-of-your-waking-hours kind of huge. Half the time we don't even know what we want to do for work when we start looking. The prospects seem endless.

Try breaking that down, too. You could sign up for a few online job boards and set a daily apply quota—like five jobs a day. That's a minimum of one-hundred jobs in one month, but when it's broken down to five jobs a day, it's way less daunting.

Take writing a book. There is no way I could put on my to-do list, "Write a damn book." That would never happen. Here's what I can do:

WEEK 1: Write Table of Contents

WEEK2: Write Introduction

WEEK 3: Write the first section (three-five pages)

WEEK 4: Write two more sections (ten pages)

Now look at it—I wrote the damn book.

If there are things you've been avoiding because they're too big, break them down into small, actionable items. The actionable part is key. Just because they're smaller doesn't mean you'll do them. It just means that now you have more things to ignore on your to do list.

If something is important to you, find the time. I bet if you broke down all the days where you've said, "I have no time to do this," you'll find the time. Sometimes it just takes visualizing it to see what's possible.

Don't let your dreams get derailed because they felt too over-whelming. Everything's within reach. You just have to be realistic that you might not pole vault straight to your dreams. Sometimes you need a ladder.

LET PEOPLE UNDERESTIMATE YOU

When I was twenty-five, I was working in a position that was traditionally held by guys. I was heading a department that was just me. I was an island of one.

One day a few months into this position, a freelancer at the company came into my office looking bewildered. After a moment of standing in the doorway, he said, "I'm looking for the post-production office," to which I responded, "That's me." He looked around for a second, confirming he was in the right room. After a weird moment of silence, he said, "Oh, I was expecting a guy."

Now, I don't think he meant anything by this. I think he had an image in his head of who would be sitting behind my desk and that image wasn't a five-foot-tall lady. His response was likely accidental. He hadn't considered the possibility that being both a girl and in charge of the post production department aren't mutually exclusive things.

At this point, I had been underestimated or misjudged plenty of times, but I had learned long before this moment that none of that was about me—it was about the person doing the misjudging. My not being a guy had nothing to do with me, and everything to do with this person's expectations.

The week I started my first job as a producer, a few of my coworkers and I went out for drinks. There were about seven of us in the Uber when one of my new coworkers said something, to which I replied with a witty quip. He blurted out, "Oh shit. You're funny." I knew that. In certain moments I'm even hilarious. He had assumed that in the five days he'd known me, he had figured me out. I had not yet been funny around him, so therefore I couldn't be funny. People love labels and once they think they've figured you out, they label you as that thing and have a hard time switching gears.

People will always underestimate you. We're taught to draw conclusions quickly—about things, about places, about people. We're shown endless commercials that are fifteen or thirty seconds long and asked to draw conclusions about a certain product based on a limited amount of information. We scroll through social media feeds to draw conclusions on a person within seconds based on one or two photos.

You will never stop being underestimated. You will always be judged. It's human nature to judge. What I've chosen to do is to let people judge me. I know who I am; I know what I am capable of. If I get to continuously surprise people, even better. There's great satisfaction in people thinking you can't do something and proving them wrong.

SEEK A STATE OF FLOW

Don't you love those moments where you're working on a project for a quick minute, something you enjoy but don't usually have time for, and then you look up and five hours have somehow passed? In these moments you feel accomplished, you feel lighter. The rest of the world completely slipped away, and you didn't even realize it had been raining for the past hour.

That's a state of flow.

Flow states happen when we get laser focused on projects—typically ones we enjoy or have a tight deadline on. But how do we find a state of flow when we need to complete tasks that aren't as enjoyable?

Part of it will come from having a routine that motivates you. Whether it's waking up early, exercising before important activities to get the adrenaline going, or playing music and having a little dance party, do whatever it is that gets your blood pumping. It's hard to go from chilling on the couch to being so fully engaged in an activity that the world around you fades. It's possible, but extremely challenging to achieve without a routine.

You know the result you want—you want to bang out some important shit and come out the other side knowing you've created a work of pure genius. The challenge is getting from point A to point B.

Here are a few things that work for me:

ACCOUNTABILITY
This has been highly effective for me in finding motivation. I hate the idea of letting someone else down. Even with personal projects

I'm doing that have no deadline, I'll tell friends that I'm sharing something with them at the end of the day and want their thoughts. This keeps me accountable. With this book, even though I wrote it alone, when I felt myself losing the motivation to write, I told more friends that I was writing a book and their feedback made me inspired again.

MUSIC

Blasting fun music and dancing around helps get me motivated and into a state of flow. Sometimes playing music makes me clean the house better. Sometimes I find that I've listened to a whole album while doing a project and didn't even notice.

SHUT OFF THE INTERNET

This one sounds weird, but I find that I get distracted very easily. I have an app that lets me blacklist websites, like social media websites or news outlets I like to read, for a specified amount of time. Sometimes I find I've somehow, mindlessly typed in Facebook.com to the search bar while trying to focus on something else, so I blacklist Facebook for two hours. You can also just disconnect the Internet entirely if you're only connected through Wi-Fi. Don't worry, it'll still be there when you're done. Just limit your distractions by removing the option. If I space out and come to with my phone in my hand, I know it's time to put my phone in the other room.

TIME OF DAY

This matters more than you might think. I know myself by now—I'm most effective first thing in the morning, after a cup of coffee. Then, around mid-to-late morning, I experience a lull in productivity. I can get very productive in the late afternoon, and then in the evening my productivity tends to skyrocket. If I want to accomplish important tasks, I know to schedule them for 9:00 a.m. or around 5:00 p.m. Midday tasks aren't as enjoyable to me.

It may take some time but eventually, you'll find something that can drop you into your state of flow. The best way to find it is to start by doing something you love, whatever that may be, and take notice of when things click for you. When time starts to fly and you're really powering through things, zero in on the elements that helped make your state of flow happen and try to reproduce them later to see if they work again. That could be your golden ticket to finding your flow whenever you need it.

LOVE DOING NOTHING

I was once watching a documentary series about wild animals. The filmmakers used these high-tech cameras to capture incredible images of wild animals across the world—it's footage that's completely unfiltered, natural, and unadulterated by human interference. It's breathtaking.

I was watching one episode, about a beautiful lioness and her cubs, and the only thing I could think of was, "How can she lay around all day napping and doing nothing? She must be so bored." I doubt she's concerned with boredom, but that's where my mind goes.

I even think similar things about my dog. We go for a walk two or three times a day. He eats, lays in the sun, and takes endless naps, but whenever I get the opportunity to take him somewhere, even a quick run to the dry cleaner, I do it because I think he must want something different than his normal routine. That's me putting my own fears and anxieties of being unproductive on my dog. How insane is that?

I was never good at doing nothing. I can get about ten seconds into just sitting before I reach for my phone, turn on the TV, play some music, go for a walk, start cleaning. Something. I have to always be doing something, at least if I'm awake. I can never just be.

This level of constant activity has made me unable to relax.

Two summers ago, I decided to go to a resort in St. George, Utah to unwind for a long weekend. It's an all-inclusive resort with all meals, yoga classes, and hikes included. The perfect setup for a relaxing weekend. The entire purpose of this trip was to travel completely alone to a resort that I'd been to before and loved, so I could de-stress and fully relax. When I got there, I checked in, put on a swimsuit, and headed down to the pool. I swam for about twenty minutes, then I stretched out on a giant pool chair, under the beautiful late spring sun, and started listening to music. Ah, finally, relaxation. Then my phone died. The room was too far to walk all the way back just for a charger and the sun would be setting within the hour anyways so why bother.

Panic set in. I was sitting beside a gorgeous pool, looking out at a view of picturesque red rocks surrounding me at every angle –and I was anxious. I had no music, no book, and the pool was too cold to get back into. The late May weather was perfect, and the scenery was idyllic. I still couldn't let go. My body was having an adverse reaction to doing nothing.

The rest of the weekend was much of the same. I'd go for a hike and sit on top of a beautiful mountain but after two minutes of looking out at the view, I'd begin my hike back down. I'd lay in a hammock, feeling the light breeze every so often, but I had to have a book with me to feel comfortable relaxing.

How could I not be good at this? I'd practiced Vedic meditation before. I'd always loved hiking and taking walks, but I'd never done nothing. All of those things, while relaxing, still meant doing something.

By the time I got back home, I was convinced the weekend had been a complete waste of time. I never felt relaxed, it wasn't as good as I was expecting, and I was totally disappointed. Then I realized the reason I didn't love it was me. I had an expectation of the level of relaxation I would achieve but because I don't actually know how to relax when doing nothing, I couldn't reach that level.

This brought about a wave of epiphanies. I couldn't recall the last time I had been relaxed doing absolutely nothing. The last time I had sat on a beach alone and just looked out at the water. The last time I had watched a sunset out of my kitchen window without any distractions around me.

I started carving out five minutes a day to do nothing. I know. Counterintuitive to plan to do nothing, but it was the only way my Type A brain was ever going to learn.

I would put my phone in another room, turn off the TV, and just be. At first it sucked. I was focused on the sounds of cars around me and I kept thinking of things I should be doing.

After a while, it got more comfortable, and before long, I loved it. Now, whenever possible before bed, I go and sit outside and just look at the stars. I've found it's the perfect way to unwind from the day. I don't bring my phone; I don't put on music. Sometimes I'll be out there one minute, sometimes it's half an hour. I got comfortable with the nothingness. And through that, I learned how to relax— just being me.

Give It A Fucking Shot

- ☐ Find five minutes today to do nothing.

- ☐ Turn off all devices and put your phone in another room so you aren't tempted.

- ☐ Find a comfortable spot with no distractions.

- ☐ Try not to spend the entire time thinking of things you can do later or mentally planning dinner. Try to just enjoy the moment around you without judgment or a plan for what's next.

TAKE A MENTAL HEALTH DAY

When I was younger and final exams were looming or life was getting too heavy for my pre-pubescent brain, my mom would propose a mental health day. Typically with less than twenty-four hours' notice.

I grew up outside of Washington D.C., and one of the many joys of living in that area is you're close to a lot. We would take a day off school and go into the city to visit museums. We'd head into Philadelphia or New York City and just wander around, looking in shop windows.

It worked because it was unexpected. I didn't plan to take a day off, so it mattered in a different way than getting a free day I had planned. Plus, no one expected anything of me. On weekends, friends would've called me to hang out or I would've had chores and other activities, but nothing was scheduled on mental health days.

I basically got a day off from my life.

I kept this practice as an adult. I often do it towards the end of the year. In California, businesses offer six sick days a year, but they usually don't rollover to the following year; so if you haven't taken them, you lose them. I hate to lose stuff, so I take them. If I haven't used all of my sick days, work has been busy and life is starting to feel like a lot, I take a mental health day.

I call in sick, likely the night before, so the company has time to prepare. I just tell them I'm taking a sick day and will be unavailable. I send an email to the person taking over with everything they'll need to know. Then, I get away. Maybe I drive into the woods and go for a hike or drive to the beach and watch the waves.

I do whatever it takes to get away from my normal routine, find a place where no one knows me, and have what feels like a spontaneous vacation, even if it's twenty minutes away. I go alone. I don't tell anyone where I'm going, and I let go of every idea of accountability and responsibility for one day.

The emails will still be there when I get back. All of the standard duties of life will still be there.

Mental health is still health. It's important to make sure we don't wait until we're on the verge of a mental breakdown to take care of ourselves.

POWER DOWN

Have you ever been working all day on your computer and then it just suddenly freezes? It won't do anything, despite your furious clicking all over the place. The only way to get it to work is by turning it off and turning it back on again. Then suddenly, it's fine.

Do that for your brain. When you feel like you can't think straight, you're wandering between rooms unsure of what you're even looking for, or you're finding yourself searching for simple words in a conversation as if you're short-circuiting, it's time to power down.

Your brain is working non-stop, all day. Even when you're just laying down watching TV, it's still receiving all the audio and visual information coming at you. It needs a break.

It's hard to be in complete nothingness and give your brain a true, 100% break, but there are things you can do to minimize the amount of information it has to process at any given moment. If you're a multitasking fiend and are constantly doing five things at once, it might be too much for your brain to handle. Try slowing down and doing one thing at a time. Just like a computer, if you have too many programs open at once, you're going to crash.

Even if you don't have a whole day you can take off for a mental health day, that doesn't mean you should keep going until you collapse. Close some of the programs. Of course, you have some non-negotiable stuff you have to get done today; but be realistic—you can push something to tomorrow without consequences, right?

I'm the person whose eyes are barely open while I'm washing dishes because I can't go to bed with a sink full of dirty plates, even if I've been awake for over twenty hours and am running on fumes. It's important to recognize that unwinding for a few minutes is more important than the minor things I've decided are randomly extremely urgent.

I think back to when I was a kid and my parents would tell me it was time to go to bed, so I'd launch into my well-practiced routine of begging for "five more minutes." Somehow that translated to my adult life, only now I'm pleading with myself for five more minutes and it isn't even for fun stuff like video games. It's answering emails and straightening up the house. There's no parent yelling at me from another room, "Go the bed," so I find that, more often than not, I'm pushing myself to the limit.

Allow yourself the time and space to refuel. Take half an hour and reboot. Go for a walk. Take a nap, or just close your eyes for a few minutes. Meditate. Stretch. Get up, walk away from your work, and disconnect for a moment.

Once you do, you'll come back completely refreshed, rebooted, and ready to refocus.

EMPTY YOUR TRASH CAN

I had a teacher once describe stress as pushing tissues into a trash can. Think about a waste bin in your house right now. Picture it when you have just a few tissues in it and it hardly looks full. Then slowly, over the course of time, it fills up with more and more tissues and before you know it, it's overflowing.

Now if you're the Mother Teresa of cleaning homes, you probably go and empty the trash can. I assume most people, however, are like me and just squish the tissues down in the trash can to make room. Then I pile more on and repeat the process until there is no denying the trash needs to get taken out.

This is true in a lot of things. Laundry baskets. Plastic bag storage. Our minds.

Wait, our minds? Yup. That's stress. Instead of dealing with things, we just squish them down.

Your thought process might go something like this: "Okay, I have six things I need to deal with right now, but I can't think about them, so I'll just put them somewhere deep in my mind and go about my day. Oh wait, there's four more. Okay, put those back there too. Oh wait, forgot about that other thing." By the end of the day we're exhausted, and we can't figure out why. Then we start the whole next day and add more and more to our trash can.

You know why this isn't helpful? You never emptied the trash can from the day before. People stress themselves out so much that they can't wait to get on vacation to dump out the bin only to come back and fill it back up again.

So, here's your homework. Take two things out of the trash can today. Just two. Then two more tomorrow.

Been meaning to make a dentist appointment? Need to cancel a subscription service? Keep forgetting to call that childhood friend and catch up? Maybe you need to literally take out the trash that's been sitting in the garage for weeks. Whatever it is, deal with it.

This isn't just true for action items. It's true for those things you've been avoiding in your mind. When you squish down every thought that you don't want to deal with today, you're squishing down your mental trash can. When someone was rude to you, when someone cut you off in traffic, when your friend said something passive aggressive, and all you did was think, "Well, I don't have time to think about that right now," and moved past it, you filled up your trash can.

Unpleasant thoughts are going to come up, but when we don't deal with them, when we don't take out the trash, and we just squish them further into our subconscious, they begin overflowing into other things, like our dreams.

Try to give yourself a few minutes today to think through the things that got to you. See if you can work through a few of them. You don't have to empty the whole trash can, just take out a few pieces and see how good it feels.

Give It A Fucking Shot

☐ Pick a few items that have been on your mental to-do list for way too long and check them off this week.

☐ Take a few minutes to relax and think through the things in your head you've been avoiding—the things causing you stress. Just let the thoughts come and don't push them back down. Let them work their way out.

MAKE A BIG DEAL OF THINGS
THAT MATTER

Storytime, kids. Grab a blanket and get comfy.

In 2013, I started having neck and shoulder pain daily. Like when a toddler constantly asks mundane questions, it was a constant, annoying, and dull pain but not so debilitating that it stopped my daily life. Then came the neuropathy—a tingling or numbness in my fingers sometimes, or at the base of my neck. My pain and neuropathy landed me in the emergency room a few times over the course of the year, but each time the doctors found no cause and sent me home. After half a dozen doctors and three dozen tests, I was told there was nothing wrong with me so I tried to carry on with my life, thinking, "I guess this is just who I am now." In 2014, my thick-headed dog broke my nose and I needed surgery on it. After the surgery, my nose ran 24/7 like it was competing with Niagara Falls. I saw even more doctors and more specialists, all who said, "There's nothing wrong," as a way to avoid saying, "We have no fucking idea what's wrong with you." I found a nose spray that calmed my runny nose. I learned to adjust.

A few months after my nose surgery, I started getting migraines. First a couple of times a week, then a couple of times a day. One day around Christmas, while watching Disney's Frozen like a perfectly normal twenty-five-year-old alone in her apartment, I got so dizzy I could barely stand. This dizziness lasted on and off for weeks until shortly after New Year's, I ended up in the emergency room for the second time in ten days. They had tested me for spinal fluid leaks, organ failure—everything they could think of. They put me in touch with a neurologist who successfully found a treatment for the migraines and sent me on my way.

In 2016, I started getting over heated and having extreme skin reactions out of nowhere. I saw even more doctors and had even more tests. I was tested for pituitary, thyroid and adrenal cancers. I did Chelations to remove heavy metals, like aluminum, from my body and tried various alternative medicine treatments. Nothing worked perfectly but everything combined slowly lessened my discomfort.

Over the course of four years, I saw over twenty-five specialists, had over one hundred vials of blood drawn, two CT scans, two MRIs, and no answers. Most doctors I saw, after waiting months for an appointment, took one look at my chart, spent five minutes examining me, told me I was imagining what was wrong with me, and left the room. Their egos were too fragile to take on an unsolvable case. Their bank accounts would prefer a high quantity of easy-to-solve patients to taking time with tough-to-solve patients. This wasn't true for all of them, but most. I got used to doctors being dismissive, but I kept at it. I chose not to accept that each new thing was part of my life. I was frustrated and ready for answers. I knew there had to be a connection and I was going to cause a fuss until someone figured it out.

I started doing research before appointments and walked into new doctor's offices asking for certain tests. I made spreadsheets comparing test results, printed them out and brought them to each appointment, asking the doctor to see if there was any connection. If a doctor dismissed me after spending less than the average commercial break time examining me, I asked them to spend another minute thinking it over with me. I didn't take, "You're fine," for an answer anymore. I so clearly wasn't.

Finally, my neurologist and rheumatologist took the time to dig deeper. They worked together, alongside my fabulous new primary care doctor, and found that I had some form of an autoimmune disorder. They realized I had nerves working overtime in my body, attacking problems that weren't there. When one thing would happen, like a migraine, instead of my body deploying the regular immune battalion to go fight that thing, they would deploy the entire army and cause a full-on civil war. My body no longer knew if it was fighting the migraine causing enemies or the immune response team and would get stuck in a cycle of fighting itself. My nerves were blindly attacking anything they saw as a threat, even if it was my own, healthy cells. My body became the drunk dude in a bar fight who starts swinging at his own friend who's trying to break up the fight just because he's in combat-mode.

The doctors figured out a treatment plan and for the first time since 2013, these ailments, while not gone, have become manageable and live in the background of my otherwise kickass life. They no longer define me or consume me. That never would have happened if I didn't make a big deal of it. If I had just accepted my fate as a rapidly deteriorating person, I would likely be living some other life entirely. I kept on pushing forward. Even when I felt like giving up.

When we're little, we're taught to sit quietly in class. As we grow up, we're taught we're supposed to be polite, quiet, and easygoing. We're taught not to get angry or make a fuss because then we won't be likable. It's likely why we see people blowing up at gas station attendants or department store clerks on the regular in viral videos. These people are frustrated about something else in their lives, but they can't tell the person they need to, or at least they think they can't, so they take it out on someone else. Someone they'll never see again.

Frustrations only build. Anger only grows. Even if you think something has passed, it could come back later in a different way.

Sometimes, you have to make a big deal of something. Not every-thing and likely not even most things. Just the things that are super important and matter to you. If you're up until 4:00 a.m. thinking about an interaction with a coworker, replaying all the things you should have said, stewing in how they angered you—bring it up. Resolve it. If not, tensions will only grow and suddenly you'll be the crazy employee who screamed at the coffee machine in the break room.

The trick is *how* to make a big deal of it. I don't mean walk into the office the next day and shoot off a confetti cannon with a banner that says "'Lisa was a bitch to me yesterday." I mean that you should approach things respectfully but don't let them slide.

Things that are majorly affecting your life deserve attention. If you'll forget about it in ten minutes, like someone bumping into you in the grocery store, then sure, ignore it like you do Bed, Bath & Beyond coupons. But if your life is going to be altered by sweeping it under the rug; then don't. Put the broom away and grab your megaphone.

If someone is harassing you, don't brush it off as, "Oh well, that's just who they are." If that person is like that with you, they're probably like that with other people. Make a big deal about it.

If we as a society talked about workplace harassment like vegans talk about being vegan (no offense, vegans), we would have this problem solved by now.

We're groomed to believe that an appropriate response to all problems is, "No big deal." We're always ready with a, "No worries," or, "No problem," uttering them at strangers ten times a day like an autoreply. That's not always the case. Start identifying the things that truly bother you and speak up. Otherwise, you'll find yourself starring in a viral video screaming at someone who doesn't deserve it.

PUT THE PAST DOWN

I'm going to admit something very embarrassing to you. It's cool though; we know each other pretty well by now.

In 2017 a song came out called "Best On" by Luca and Tei Shi. Like many songs before it, I misheard the lyrics. I thought the line was, "Wait a minute, let me put my *past down*." Instead of what it actually was: "Wait a minute, let me put my *best on*." Even after I learned the real lyrics, the original ones kept rolling around in my head.

I had just ended a long relationship and was finding dating pretty hard. Something about that line, or at least what I thought it was, was telling me that I couldn't date successfully because I was still carrying the weight of my past with me. Not just my past with this specific relationship but my past in general. I had been carrying around all my previous relationships, including my approach to relationships, from high school and college, none of which served my current self. I was also carrying any baggage from my childhood that told me I wasn't good enough for certain people or certain relationships.

You've lived X number of years and because of that, you've accumulated some shit. You don't mean to, but you're carrying it around. It's why we still cringe when we think of that embarrassing thing we did in fourth grade.

The past is super heavy. It's every moment of your life up to this point. You're not carrying *all* of those moments around with you, but I'd bet you're still carrying ones you don't need anymore.

That time you pissed off your roommate Freshman year of college. She's forgotten about it (or she hasn't—who cares, it's in the past). Put it down.

That minor car accident you caused when pulling out of a parking spot without looking both ways. The cars are fixed, everyone's fine. Put it down.

That time you yelled at your mom and you got in a big fight. It's fine. She's your mom and she loves you. Put it down.

You aren't done living yet. You're going to continue to pile on more memories and more things to carry around. Do you really want the weight you're carrying to get heavier? Practice unloading some unnecessary baggage. Whenever a thought creeps in that no longer serve you, acknowledge it, laugh about it, and move on. Don't sit and stew in it. It's in the past; move forward.

HEARING NO ISN'T A BAD THING

When you're a kid, "no" is a vital part of learning. It teaches you boundaries. It teaches you respect and how to take rejection. It teaches you that sometimes shit doesn't go your way and that's okay. Then we grow up. Suddenly we no longer have the capacity to hear "no" because it feels personal or unwelcomed.

If you're an adult who's surrounded by people who never say, "No," to you, well then, you're a politician. For everyone else, no creates balance and keeps our egos in check. You have to hear "no" to understand and respect limits.

If your partner agreed to everything you wanted, then there would be no balance in your relationship. One person—you—would call all the shots. They aren't saying, "No," to hurt you, they're saying, "No," to ensure their voice is heard too and you're in an equal partnership. It's good when someone challenges you because it holds you accountable to not always getting your way.

If someone tells us, "No" and we take it personally, we have to examine why. If I ask my boss if I can take on a specific project and they say, "No," I have to look at why. Or even ask why. Do they not think my skills match the level required for this project? Do they think I have too much on my plate already? Is there someone else more qualified for it?

"No" helps us improve. If the answer to the above scenario is that they don't think I'm skilled enough for this project, I better go learn some new skills.

"No" can feel like a blow to the chest sometimes. When you ask someone out on a date and they say, "No," it can feel like you've been cut to your core. That "no" is a blessing though, because it opens you up to dating people who want to be with you, who are excited at the prospect.

When you asked your parents for something as a child, like a toy, and they said, "No," you likely threw a fit for a minute but then got over it. You learned that you could live without that toy, that you weren't entitled to have everything, that there are limits on the things you can buy or have, and that you should cherish the things you already have for those reasons.

Sure, your child brain probably didn't pick up on those lessons at the time and was super pissed but look at the awesome person you are now.

And look at the shitty people who were spoiled as kids and were never told, "No." They've become the movie villain or the stereotypical hot head at work. Those people are honestly miserable because they've convinced themselves the world is against them when really, the world just caught up to them.

Be thankful for the "no." It keeps you grounded in what you have and prevents you from being a total asshole.

CLOSE SOME TABS

At the end of 2019, the comedian Hasan Minhaj gave a monologue about how to survive 2020 in the current political and social climate of America. Oh, Hasan. If only you knew what 2020 would bring.

The main thing I took away from this monologue was his concept of "Close Some Tabs."

> "We're exposed to all the news all the time, which makes us feel like we have to care about everything all the time," Hasan says, "Give yourself a break. Just pick a couple things to not care about, for your sanity. I'm not saying shut down your browser, just close a couple tabs."

We're beyond the Twenty-Four-Hour News Cycle and now in a Twenty-Four-Hour News Onion, where every new piece of information is a layer deeper than the last and makes us want to cry. Let other people worry about some of the things you aren't extremely passionate about so you can focus on what matters to you and your sanity.

In 2020, for example, we had a lot to worry about: a pandemic, a presidential race, a slew of protests, and a very divided political climate. All of that exists on top of the usual worries like climate change and foreign unrest. We then pile on bullshit like Donald Trump's tweets, Kanye West's tweets, "Karens" going viral for being annoying and racist, Aunt Becky going to prison, and a bunch of half-baked conspiracy theories. With all the major stuff being too important, I decided to close that tier of tabs. I didn't have the energy to give a shit about an actress bribing her daughter's way into college because there were real problems in the world.

You don't have to focus on all the news all the time. How could you? You still have to go to work and live a normal life. You've got your own personal shit to worry about. If you focused on all of it, you'd be more overwhelmed than a chameleon in a skittles factory.

Closing tabs gives you the chance to zero in on the stuff that actually matters to you. I close tabs so I can focus on the things that matter most to me and my loved ones rather than being bogged down by what's trending at that moment. No matter how much the Internet wishes things were different, a Kardashian scandal will never be more important to me than a Supreme Court case. The Kardashian's will never affect my future, whereas a Supreme Court case might. At least, I hope that's true. The only thing Kris Jenner hasn't gotten around to is world domination.

So, I've instituted a barometer that I welcome you to use. When I see a news story, I ask myself, "Will this matter in a month?" If Karen going nuts in a parking lot won't matter in a month, I can't care today. I'm too busy focusing on climate change and social change to give a shit if some mom in Arkansas went on a rant about wiping down shopping carts.

So, go ahead. Do yourself a favor. Close some tabs. You'll feel better once you have.

PROTECT YOUR PEACE

Protecting your peace means that if you need a moment of peace and someone or something is compromising that for you, then remove yourself from the situation.

Easier said than done, right? It always seems like the moment I need peace the most is the moment everyone wants something from me.

When I've had an exceptionally long week, filled with endless meetings, emotional rollercoasters and what can only be described as traffic brought to earth by Satan himself, those are the weeks I have a friend who needs to vent to me for three hours on the phone.

It sometimes requires stepping away from a situation to protect your peace. You may have to remove yourself from that friend's venting session for the time being, in a gentle way, to preserve your own sanity. Say something like, "I would really love to help you with this, but it has been the world's longest week and I have to decompress tonight. Can we talk tomorrow?"

The moment your peace is about to be compromised is almost always recognizable. Your body tenses up, you may let out an involuntary sigh, and your thoughts start racing on how to get out of this situation.

A few months back I was in line at a Starbucks. I had had a long week, I was exhausted, and here I was, listening to the guy in front of me argue with the barista. The line was taking forever and he was being unrelenting to the staff who was trying to help him. I could feel my anxiety level rising. "What if I get roped into this?", I thought. Then, "Wait, should I help the poor Starbucks employees?

I don't even know what I'd do right now." So, I left. At that moment, I had to protect my peace.

Never worry about who you might be offending when you're trying to protect your peace. You can almost always set a boundary with a simple, "I don't think I can handle this right now, but let's circle back in a bit," or by just not answering the phone, not responding to the email, or getting out of line. Your peace is important, and you have the right to protect it.

I was once dating someone whose house I would spend a lot of time at. He had a yard and a bigger living space. On paper it made sense to spend a lot of our time together there. In reality, I was always around his stuff, his roommates, eating his food, listening to his favorite music, and watching his favorite movies. After a while, I found it overwhelming because it demanded constant effort. I never felt relaxed because it wasn't my space. I noticed that after about forty-eight hours, I'd start to get anxiety there. I'd get engulfed by my need for space and feel a strong desire to go home. Even at 1:00 a.m., I'd have trouble sleeping because of the itching feeling inside that I needed to wake up in my own bed.

Once I decided to honor that feeling, I started enjoying my time there more. I was acknowledging that my peace was tied to being in my space, with my stuff, listening to my own music, and as long as I had regular doses of that, I was perfectly content spending time at his house, too. I had to be okay telling him when I needed to go home and not feeling guilty about needing my own space.

Protecting your peace is protecting your sanity. Recognize the moments you're feeling overwhelmed by a situation and really listen to what your heart is telling you. If you need to remove yourself from that situation to feel at peace, do it.

"BE CAREFUL NOT TO DO SOMETHING PERMANENTLY STUPID BECAUSE YOU'RE TEMPORARILY ANGRY, STRESSED, SCARED, TIRED OR HUNGRY"

— KAREN SALMANSOHN

EVERYONE'S AN ADDICT

Remember D.A.R.E.? Man, I hope you do, otherwise I'm older than I thought. Well, D.A.R.E stands for Drug Abuse Resistance Education. It was a program that taught us that addictions come in two forms: drugs and alcohol (somehow not the A in D.A.R.E). As much as it pains me to say it, D.A.R.E. was wrong. I'm "addicted" to coffee and travel. I'm also addicted to not feeling sadness. When I feel sad, I will do literally anything I can to not feel that way. I'll distract myself from my feelings, which isn't healthy, but is likely at the root of most of the world's addictions.

Everyone's an "addict." We sometimes find it really easy to judge other people for their addictions when they require twelve-step programs or external interventions, but I have yet to meet a single person in my life who isn't addicted to something. That's because everyone has emotions and everyone has found ways to deal with those emotions.

This chapter is not to diminish the hardships of addicts in recovery programs. There are some people whose addictions reach an unhealthy level and who need outside assistance in order to regain their happiness and well-being. Those people are incredibly strong for picking up and rebuilding and I admire them for doing so.

This chapter is rather meant to dig into how we use lesser, more socially acceptable addictions to distract ourselves from our true, buried emotions.

First, we have to recognize what an addiction is—it's a pattern of behavior we're unwilling to change. Our addictions can come from shame, guilt, and/or regret—all those fun emotions mentioned in the *Guilt And Regret Are Useless Emotions* chapter—or they're there to soothe us. Whatever the reason, they represent an emotional response to something we're feeling.

Let's further examine my addiction to coffee. I can't imagine my life without it. I am fully convinced that coffee is a necessary element in my daily life to keep me happy. It's my escape, however momentary. Even on a day that feels shitty, if I've had my coffee, it feels like I've been soothed in a way that makes me content with the present moment. I don't have to deal with the emotions making me feel shitty. All addictions are manifestations of people seeking to feel good— about themselves, about life, about the world in general.

If we focused on "healthy" addictions as much as we focused on unhealthy ones, we might actually get to the root of why people get stuck in these patterns. Just because one person drinks seven glasses of whiskey every day, and another person runs seven miles every day—it doesn't mean that either person is less sad. It just means they have different approaches to handling uncomfortable feelings.

If you're reading this chapter thinking you're not an addict at all, it's possible. Maybe you're so incredibly in tune with your feelings that you don't cling to things to feel better. It's also possible it just isn't showing up like you think it will. It's showing up as an hour-long online shopping session after a crap phone call or binge-watching Seinfeld for the twelfth time when you're longing for childhood comforts. It's that sigh of relief you feel the second you hit the Instagram app icon even though you've promised yourself you'd delete the account. I promise myself constantly I'll delete Facebook. Then I find the comfort in ten minutes a day where I'm scrolling through a newsfeed, trading in my own life's experience for other people's. I can escape into the highlight reel of other lives while ignoring anything beyond my phone.

Ignoring your addictions won't make them go away. Denying them won't make the emotions they're covering any less present. Address the emotional components under the surface and see what aspects of your normal routine feel less necessary.

Give It A Fucking Shot

☐ For the next week, spend thirty minutes a day just sitting with your feelings. No judgments, no pushing things away. Just sit and practice feeling what you need to feel.

☐ After a week of this practice, notice what habits have faded away. Those are your addictions.

☐ If you're struggling with a serious or unhealthy addiction, seek help. SAMHSA is a great place to start (1-800-662-HELP).

SEEK HUMOR

I love to laugh. Once in school, I was prompted to answer, "What's your favorite hobby," and I wrote, "Laughing." It's hands-down my favorite thing to do. It makes me happy; it connects me with others in a way nothing else can, and it provides me relief on tough days. If that's not the definition of a hobby, I don't know what is.

I gravitate towards comedic movies and TV shows, I love watching stand-up comedy, and fill my life with hilarious friends. Humor is the fastest way to my heart and the quickest way to change my mood. Well, that and pasta.

My dad used to say I had a remarkable ability to go from sobbing uncontrollably to laughing hysterically within half a second. He was right. It's because humor is my catchall cure. There is nothing in the entire universe that can heal me in a way that laughter can. It's the free, instant cure to any shitty mood.

I have a board on Pinterest that's filled with hilarious photos and memes. I also have a YouTube playlist that's filled with TV show bloopers and hilarious videos of animals. If I'm not feeling like myself, I play one of these videos and it works every time to get me laughing; even if I've seen the same video fifty times already. Who says humor has to be momentary and spontaneous? It's magic that you can capture in a bottle and access whenever you need.

Laughter changes your mood whether you want it to or not. Have you ever seen someone trip and fall? People freeze, waiting to see how the person reacts. When they start laughing at how ridiculous that moment was, it eases the tension for everyone else.

If you're stuck in a negative headspace and you can't find your way out—seek humor. Laughter triggers the release of endorphins, which literally make your body feel good. Even smiling gets you part of the way there by releasing dopamine into your brain to tell your brain you're happy.

Life gets so serious that sometimes we need to remind ourselves that we deserve to laugh daily. You don't have to be happy to feel happy. You just have to trick your brain. In my experience the fastest way to fake it until you make it is to seek humor, so start Googling funny cat videos.

Give It A Fucking Shot

☐ Think back to the last time you laughed. The kind of laughter where you got a cramp in your side and peed a little. Got it?

☐ Now boil that moment down to what it was that made you laugh? A joke? A video? A cute puppy?

☐ Find ways to recreate that and then find ways to have it at your fingertips. If a cute puppy on the sidewalk did something hilarious that made you laugh, bookmark videos of puppies doing something similar. If a comedian made a joke you laughed at for ten minutes, save all their standup specials to re-watch later.

YOU ARE ENOUGH

Do you have any idea of the journey you took to get here? No, really. I mean one random egg and one sperm joined and you were born. You did the rest. You learned how to breathe. You learned how to laugh. Then you learned how to eat, how to stand on your own two feet, how to walk, how to talk, how to write.

You learned how to make friends. You learned right from wrong. You learned how to be kind. You learned everything they taught you in school and tons of stuff they didn't. Everything you know right now, you learned.

You learned how to be strong. You learned how to heal. You learned how to handle everything life has thrown your way up to this very moment. You learned what was worth your time. You learned what risks were worth taking. You learned your own worth. You learned how to rebound from failure.

Are you fucking kidding me? That's way more than enough. Look at all the stuff you've already done, and that's not even including the specific stuff that makes you unique. You're skilled in so many things. You're valued for so many reasons.

That's so much more than enough. That's fucking magic.

That's all this chapter is for. To remind you that you are goddamn SPECTACULAR.

PART FOUR

LIFE
SHIT

TRAVEL ON ANY BUDGET

"The world is a book, and those who do not travel
read only a page."
Saint Augustine

You don't have to wait to have the fancy job, the guy, the girl, the
family, the fat wallet, or the full life in order to travel. There are tons
of ways to travel and see the world right now. Tomorrow's never
guaranteed, and money always returns. Time never does.

I traveled a lot as a kid with my parents, but didn't really consider
traveling out of the country as an adult since I didn't make a ton of
money with my first few jobs. When I was in my mid-twenties, I was
hanging out with a friend and we read an article about something
called *Kayak Explore*. There are now several websites with similar
features, but the concept is this: you put in your budget, departure
location, and dates, and the search engine finds something that fits
your parameters.

We decided to give it a try. Los Angeles to Anywhere. $500 round-
trip. It was around November, and we were feeling spontaneous,
so we selected "winter" to see what would come up. There it was.
LAX to Copenhagen—$340 roundtrip. After picking seats, meals,
and checked bags, our fare come out to just under $500. It ended up
being my friend, my boyfriend at the time, and me.

We booked it, then decided ten days in Copenhagen was probably too long in frigid January weather, so we booked half the time
in Berlin. It was an amazing decision and ignited many future

travels by simply being a proof of concept. I ended up spending less than $1000 on that trip (not including food and souvenirs). Two cities, nine nights in hostels, lots of museums, fun activities, and adventures.

You can do that, too. You deserve an adventure. Don't talk yourself out of it. Look at the options and pick a place, time frame, and price that fits the kind of adventure you're looking for. Book it. I promise you, there's always a way to make it work.

Take a page from my playbook and hop to different places to make things more fun. Maybe you're looking at a place that has a ten-day roundtrip airfare for a super reasonable price, but you don't want to spend ten days there. Look at surrounding places and see if there's cheap transportation (flight, train, rental car) to go to another place for half the time. I've done this in a few places in Europe and Asia. Most of the time, it's quite inexpensive getting around. From Copenhagen we found flights to Berlin for $70 one way and then took an overnight bus the other way for around $40. In Spain, I went to Morocco for less than $80 one way but had a layover in Paris for an hour. In Singapore, I found a three-hour bus that went to Malaysia for under $20.

Once that's booked, work on the accommodations. If you're like me, you want something nice, but it's hard to justify shelling out a lot of money on a room you'll only sleep in. If I am in a city, I know I'll spend a lot of time outside of my hotel or hostel, so I typically make a list of five or six must-see attractions in that place, map them out, and find a location pretty central to what I want to see and do.

My number one requirement is always a stellar cancelation policy. I've been known to change plans while I'm traveling and need flexibility.

Last up: the activities. I'm not a huge planner on trips, but I like to make lists of the places I want to see, the shows I'd love to get tickets to, and the restaurants I want to eat at. Then when I get there, I just pick a few things from the list to do each day. If reservations are needed, I try to make them a week or two before I arrive. For activities, some cities have packages, like a buy-one-get-one, for certain attractions. Again, cancelation policies are key.

I usually just use Wi-Fi when I travel since international rates can be expensive on cell phone plans, but for my month-long trip around Asia, I did find a cell phone carrier, called Google Fi, that offered free international text and data. It worked pretty well in most places and was much cheaper than sticking with a domestic carrier and adding international on top of my current plan.

There are always ways to cut costs and do things cheaper. You can get groceries when you land and cook at your hostel or Airbnb. You can find coupons or student discounts for some activities. There's always a way.

Then just go. Book it. Hop on the plane. Don't look back.

"A MIND THAT IS STRETCHED BY A NEW EXPERIENCE CAN NEVER GO BACK TO ITS OLD DIMENSIONS."

— OLIVER WENDELL HOLMES

TRAVEL ALONE

So now that I've (successfully) convinced you to travel right now, on whatever budget you have, I'm going to push you one step further.
Travel alone.
I know. Terrifying.
It's really not though. I really believe everyone should travel alone. On the half dozen trips I've taken alone, I've learned more about myself than anything I've come to know in my normal routine.
The first real solo trip I took was to Seattle. I had wanted to go, had gotten some recent birthday gift money, and all my friends were too busy to make the trip. I'd found a roundtrip flight for about $100 from L.A. and decided to take it. It was short—I left early Saturday morning and came back Monday afternoon, but I made the most of those forty-eight hours. I saw Pike Place, the first Starbucks, the Fremont Troll, The Space Needle, The Chihuly Garden and Glass Museum, and even saw a tour of a Broadway show. I ate at some incredible restaurants and met awesome people, typically at those restaurants since I usually sit at the bar in restaurants, making it easier to talk with other people eating alone.
That's the thing. You're never really alone. Even if you are, you get really good at being your own company. Chances are, you'll always meet people when you travel.
I often start by looking for hostels with private rooms as accommodations. This way I can easily meet people but still get the privacy of a hotel room. Hostels tend to offer group outings or have more common areas than traditional hotels. Sometimes they have

bar crawls or movie nights. I've stayed at places with wine tastings, yoga classes, family dinners, and even game nights.

If a hostel isn't your thing, find a hotel with a bar or a nice lounge area where you can meet people.

Also sign up for walking tours, cooking classes, or any group event where there will be tons of single people.

If you're shy, that's fine. You don't really have to talk with any of these people, but you still won't be alone. You'll be on a group activity with other solo traveling strangers.

When I landed in Madrid, I spent the first five hours alone. That was it. I was eating dinner at a restaurant near where I was staying when a girl about my age walked in. She was having trouble ordering due to the language barrier, so I offered to help. We both must have stuck out to the server as Americans because we were eating so much earlier than everyone else in Madrid. We got to chatting and spent the whole night laughing and hanging out.

It turned out we were staying right near each other, so we agreed to go to a jazz club nearby the next night. The night after that we saw a flamenco show. We met other people along the way and when she left town, I ended up hanging out with them. We each did our own solo thing during the day but would meet up at night for some fun around town. I also met people at museums, restaurants, and on walking tours during my time there. I left that city with twenty new people in my contact list and hundreds of wonderful new memories.

When I went to Bali, I met someone at every place I stayed. In the hotel restaurant at breakfast, an Australian woman mentioned she was going to a market nearby that I also wanted to check out, so we split a cab and ended up walking around together most of the day. Then by the pool of the next place, I met an Austrian girl who was fascinating, and we ended up trying a cool restaurant around the corner together. We shared meals a few times and even went to a speakeasy in the back of a convenience store. I also hung out with someone I had met through a Facebook group called Girls Love Travel before I had arrived. We ended up going on at least three or four adventures, including a cool hike together.

On that same trip, I went on a volcano hike with a guide and another solo traveling girl from Australia. We were so bonded by the end of the intense hike that we went to a coffee plantation and a jungle swing after.

I always find it's great to meet other solo travelers because you can help each other with silly things like taking pictures. You don't want to return home and find you only have selfies. But even if you don't make trip friends, I've got a few tricks for avoiding that.

Whenever I travel, I pack a collapsible tripod. The one I have is eight inches when folded and fits in my wristlet purse. When I want to take photos, I set up the tripod, slide my phone in it, set my phone to video, and shoot. Then later that night when I'm at dinner or in my room, I take screenshots of the photos I like. This method gives you a better shot at getting a photo you like. If you use a timer, you'll only get a few photos at most, whereas a video lets you pick the best moment out of the entire video.

I've never been very brave when it comes to asking others to take a photo of me. Even more disappointing is when I finally do ask, I get it back and the photo is horrible, or the person's thumb is covering part of it and I have to wait for them to walk away so I can ask someone else. Doing it myself is just easier. At first, I felt silly using a tripod, but eventually I stopped caring that people are watching me take photos of myself. I'll never see these people again anyways.

Sure, traveling alone has its obstacles but all those hurdles are worth it in the end. You learn who you are when you travel. You learn what you like to do. Better yet, you have no obligation to do the things you don't like because there's no one else there telling you what to do or where to go.

It's incredibly freeing to travel alone—a kind of freedom I can't explain in reference to anything else. It's like driving down a seaside highway in a convertible for days on end.

You make friendships that you'll keep forever.

You see places you probably never would've seen, and you'll see things at your own pace. You won't be stuck in a museum for four hours because your travel companion is slowing you down.

You eat the best meals because you're picking every place. You don't have to cater to anyone else's diet.

You'll never settle, because no one will be asking you to.

Try it. Start small. It's going to be scary. It's going to feel awkward at first. How could it not? You've probably never done something like it before. All new experiences can be a little awkward, but they can also turn out to be wonderfully life changing.

USE TRAVEL HACKS

As you can probably tell by now, traveling is quite a hobby of mine. It's honestly more than that. It's a passion. A lifestyle. It's so important to me, it managed to consume three chapters of this book. It's soothes my soul in ways nothing else can.

Through all my travels I've picked up quite a few tricks, a few of which I've already shared with you in the previous chapters, but I've got a bunch more that I also think are worth sharing. Hopefully, they help you on your next adventure.

PACKING
If you're anything like me, you overpack clothing and then have no room for the souvenirs you actually want when you're on the trip because of the jacket you put in your suitcase but never actually wore.

In the months leading up to a trip, I gather clothing items I'd usually plan to donate to Goodwill, and then pack them. As I go along my trip, I leave a few items at each stop along the way. A shirt and a pair of socks here, a pair of pants there; just stuff I no longer need.

Many hotels typically keep those items and add them to a lost and found or spare clothing bin (hopefully washing them first). If someone arrives and their luggage is lost or they need to borrow a pair of socks for a hike, the hotel can offer them these clothes.

The same is true for books. I love to bring physical books on vacations with me, but they take up so much space. I usually leave them in hostels at reception when I check out so they can give them to future guests.

EXCHANGING MONEY

I don't recommend exchanging much money before you leave. I only exchange enough in local currency to get me from the airport to the hotel. That means cab fare, any visa fees, enough for water or coffee when I land, and that's about it. Then when I check in, I go to a nearby ATM and get cash.

If you have a debit card with no international fees on certain ATMs, map out their locations before you arrive. For example, I have a credit union debit card that has no foreign ATM fees at 7-Elevens worldwide. If I go to Thailand, where there are 7-Elevens on every corner, I pinpoint the one nearest my hotel before I arrive so I can walk there whenever I need to.

Even if you don't have free international transactions, it's almost always cheaper to get money out of an ATM than to try and exchange beforehand. Often time exchange rates out of the country are higher than in the country and the airport exchange rates are higher than anywhere else.

Look into international cards. I have a Revolut card, which is similar to Venmo but works internationally. I can add money easily through the app and it works in several countries without international fees. Revolut converts currency within the app and gets you the current market rate.

EXTRA CASH

So you're wrapping up your fabulous two-week adventure around Paris and you've got about 10€ left. This isn't enough to exchange back but it's too much to let go to waste.

Add it to a gift card. Many places, like Starbucks, McDonalds, or even 7-Elevens will have gift cards you can add cash to. Then when you go home you can use the gift card.

If you think you might return one day to Europe, consider keeping the money for the next trip. I have a clear, decorative shadow box with a money slot that I keep all of my spare currency in. If I ever go back to a country, I grab the money out before my trip for a little extra cash along the way.

SEEK OUT REWARDS PROGRAMS

Once, I was traveling for a month around Asia and decided to commit to one hotel booking website for all my hotel accommodations. I booked over half a dozen hotels with that website during my trip, which provided me a lifetime membership to their level two rewards program, granting me a 15% booking discount for life. Many websites offer rewards programs that provide 10-15% off all bookings, free breakfasts, and even free hotel room upgrades when possible. By committing to one website for bookings, you rack up enough points to save on future trips.

GLOBAL ENTRY

This is very much a U.S.-based hack. I first signed up for global entry in 2016 and have fallen in love with it ever since. It's $100 for five years, so $20/year. Here's what you get:

1. Clear customs in mere minutes instead of waiting hours in line. This is HUGE for me. When I came back from Israel in 2014, I waited over two hours in the customs line, and that was before I got to baggage claim. I was exhausted from the long trip and just wanted to go home. Since getting Global Entry, I've never waited more than fifteen minutes to reach baggage claim. Even when I flew back from Japan in March 2020, at the height of the Covid-19 pandemic, I sailed through customs, baggage claim, and the health inspection in under an hour.
2. TSA PreCheck on domestic flights, which is especially nice during the holidays when you sail past everyone in the long security lines. Ignore their jealous looks.
3. The ability to bypass the long lines at land and sea entrances for Mexico and Canada.
4. Faster entry into various countries with

Global Entry partnership, including England, Australia, Taiwan, Singapore, Switzerland, Germany, and Argentina. Use their local "trusted traveler" lines.

The process for Global Entry is quite simple. You fill out an application online that takes about twenty minutes. Then once they email you that your application is approved, you schedule an in-person interview at your local international airport. During the interview you show your passport, proof of residence, and approval letter, and do a ten-minute interview consisting of simple questions like naming all of the countries you've traveled to in the past five years and if you have any upcoming trips. Then you take a photo and leave. You're done.

A friend of mine scheduled her interview for a day she was already flying domestically. She just scheduled it for about two hours before her flight since she was already going to be at the airport. That's next level smart.

TSA PRECHECK

If Global Entry is too much for you, consider applying for TSA PreCheck. It only applies for domestic flights but if you travel a few times a year, you'll save hours in security lines.

You don't have to take off your shoes or take electronics out of the bag. Security lines for TSA PreCheck at LAX, my usual departure airport, are typically fifteen minutes or less. Even when I flew the day before Thanksgiving, the regular security line was over an hour and I was done in ten minutes.

I advise Global Entry above TSA PreCheck because of cost. TSA PreCheck is $85 where Global Entry is $100, both for five years. If you think you may fly out of the country once in the next five years, it's well worth the extra $15.

TAKE TINY SOAPS

When I travel abroad, especially alone, I typically stay at a mixture of hotels, hostels and Airbnbs. Whenever I'm in a hotel, I grab all the tiny soaps, shampoos, and conditioners, and save them for when I'm in the hostels, which typically don't offer those types of amenities.

The same is true for laundry bags. Some hotels offer laundry bags in the closets. When they're there, I always grab them and use them for various needs throughout my trip. They can be great when hiking to put wet shoes in, or to separate out laundry when traveling between places, or even to secure water bottles in a backpack so they don't leak condensation all over my other stuff.

POINTS CARD

I have a points credit card that gave me a $500 travel reward when I spent $3000 in the first three months. I put everything imaginable on that credit card just to rack up points. Meals out with friends, groceries, online shopping—even parking meters. Anything to get those points!

With a points credit card, you usually receive points for every dollar spent and then you can later redeem those points for travel credit on flights, hotels, or transportation. For example, if I have 50,000 points on my credit card, that equals a $500 credit.

TRACK CONFIRMATION NUMBERS

You likely booked your flights and hotels weeks, if not months, before your trip. When the time comes to check in, it can be a pain to dig through your email to find the confirmation. Try favoriting, flagging, or saving these emails in a folder as they come in to make for an easier search.

If you're a mega nerd like me, you can even make a spreadsheet with all your flight and hotel confirmation numbers to print out and bring with you just in case Internet is hard to access when you get wherever you're going.

GET OFFLINE MAPS

There is an app I like called "maps.me." It allows you to download maps of the cities you're visiting so you can wander around carefree without worrying about Wi-Fi or data availability. This has been especially helpful in countries where the LTE or Wi-Fi hasn't been very strong. I would've been lost without this in the jungles of Bali.

PROTECT YOUR PRIVACY

We live in an age where things about you are available on the Internet whether you want them there or not. Like opening a pack of Starbursts and finding all lemon, it can be a real disappointment to find there isn't much you can do to control it. There are a few things you can do, however, to limit the amount of information out there. Let's focus on those things.

What You Put Out There

Think back to who you were ten years ago. Did you just cringe a little bit? Were you thinking of how awkward you were? All the weird choices you made? Now think about all the embarrassing posts you made on LiveJournal, MySpace, or whatever social media platform was cool when you were younger. Today, when I think about my online presence, I think in terms of protecting myself in ten years from that cringing feeling.

On good days, we want the world to know we're happy. We got a new job, got engaged, ate an incredible meal. There's only one problem with this mentality. When we invite the world in to celebrate the good with us, they feel entitled to the bad, too.

You got a new job and celebrated with an Instagram post. You're raking in all the likes and feeling the warm glow of the Internet love. A few months later your company hits rough times and you're let go. Now everyone you've ever talked to knows you have this job, so you'll feel obligated to explain to them what happened.

You got engaged and celebrated on social media with an epic cliff-side photoshoot. But if down the road, you get divorced, all your friends who liked and commented on that engagement post are going to want to know what happened. That may be the last thing you want in a tough time like that.

I've learned this lesson the hard way. I was very public once with a long-term relationship. When that ended, I didn't announce it. I did, however, have to endure years of run-ins with people from the past asking, "How's your guy?"

Take a lesson from Britney Spears. In 2007, the world watched her melt down after they had spent years watching her climb to the top. "Britney Spears" was now associated with the phrases "mess" and "train wreck." I hated how everyone turned on her based on a few pictures from a hair salon. That was not how I wanted the Internet to treat me. I learned to be careful with what I shared because clearly people were just as interested in building you up as they were with tearing you down.

When I post something, I have a few thoughts first:

"Does this need to be shared? Will people following my page benefit from it?"

"Will there be any kickback? If this starts a fight, is it one I want to have and will be proud of having in a year?"

"Does this pass the future cringe-proof test?"

I'm not saying don't share. Just institute some basic protocols.

KEEP YOUR PRIVACY SETTINGS HIGH
Don't make anything public you wouldn't want your worst enemy to see. Sometimes Googling privacy settings for various social media platforms points you to privacy features you didn't even know about.

KEEP YOUR FRIENDS CLOSE

Don't friend anyone who you don't know personally or trust. This is the basic stranger-danger rule we learned in kindergarten. It still applies even after we've learned to cross the street by ourselves.

KEEP YOUR POSTS SCARCE

Be careful what you post. Not just for safety but for your future self. Think of every conversation you'll have to have if this post goes sideways. Your friends can never un-see a post. Neither can your enemies. There's also the added value that people won't get sick of seeing a dozen posts of you a day. If you only post every now and then, people will be more excited when you do share something.

DON'T FIGHT

Don't get involved in social media battles. You'll never know which coworkers, friends of your parents, or long-lost relatives are following the same public page and the same thread. The Internet is written in ink and things cannot be undone, even if you delete them.

DON'T SHARE YOUR ADDRESS

When meeting someone in person that you met online, do so in a public space and never share your address. With that said, also Google their phone number or email to see if there are any public red flags before you meet. A quick phone number search might just show you if they ever did some shady shit, like tried to sell toenail clippings on Craigslist.

DON'T CLICK LINKS

Don't click links you can't be positive are meant for you. You can end up spamming everyone you've ever emailed and ruining a lot of people's day. If you aren't sure if something is meant to be opened, you can always reply and ask. I've definitely received emails from friends with no subject line and just a link. In those cases, I reply, "Did you mean to send this to me? Just checking before I click it." You can also check the URL in the email address. If something looks like it's from Google but came from info@googlerocks.com, it's not from Google.

CHECK WITH YOUR FRIENDS

Ask your friends before tagging them. This is more just common courtesy than safety. You don't want someone posting a photo of you on a bad hair day where you look drunk, but told your boss you were home sick so you could go to a concert.

This is especially true for children. When I was in Indonesia, I saw a group of tourists take a photo of a child playing on the floor of a store where her mother worked and post the photo to Instagram. That's not okay. They didn't ask the mother if they could put her child on the Internet, nor did they show any hesitation in doing so. It's unfortunately becoming normal to post random children on the Internet and it needs to stop. I even watched a Netflix series where a girl moves to Paris and within the first episode meets an au pair friend and posts to social media a photo of the two children this woman watches. How would that mother like it if she was online one day and saw a photo of her child? Upon reaching a certain age, a kid can decide for themselves if they're cool with their photo being on the Internet, but before then it should be left up to the parent.

What You Don't Put Out There but Definitely Exists Anyway:

GOOGLE YOURSELF

Have you ever Googled yourself and realized there was a ton of info about you that you don't want out there? Even better, have you ever Googled your name and then your city or street name to find your address, phone number, and real age is public knowledge? If you scroll down to the contact page, some of these sites let you put in requests to have it removed.

PEOPLE LOVE TO TAG
You may be tagged in things and not even know it. Some social media websites let you type in your name and see what posts you're mentioned in. You can do the same thing in Google news or Google images. If there's something you don't want out there, flag it for removal.

DATA BREACH
You may have had your info stolen. Be very careful where you purchase things online. Only enter your credit card and personal info into websites that are secure (look for a padlock symbol in the address bar). If your info is stolen, cancel your credit card immediately.

Overall, just be smart. Don't say anything online you wouldn't say to your boss in person. Don't post your address unless you want to invite a ton of sketchy people to your house. Protect your future self by thinking through the things you post online.

The Internet is only getting weirder. Keep yourself protected from the strange.

GIVE TO CHARITY

Nothing bad has ever happened when someone donated to charity. Sure, some people froze their asses off for an ice bucket challenge but beyond that, nothing goes wrong when you donate to a legitimate charity. Only good things happen. There are the obvious benefits (you're improving other people's lives) but there are also less obvious, more *you*-centric, benefits. Let's discuss those.

To start, when you donate to charity, you're eligible for a tax deduction. Remember those deductions from the first section? You can owe less in federal taxes by deducting expenses, including charitable donations. That's just a nice little something to keep in mind if you're looking for a benefit.

Donating causes a ripple effect. Not just for the world, but for you. We all accidentally become selfish. We get busy, work takes over, family monopolizes our time, and we suddenly forget that there are people in the world outside of our bubble. Donating your money, your time, your clothing—whatever it may be—gives you a moment to see outside yourself. You're suddenly in the world beyond your usual circle. Whether you're conscious of it or not, you start to look at things differently.

Maybe you donate your time one day to help clean up a beach, then a few weeks later you donate clothing you no longer wear, then a week or two later, you see a foundation you support holding an online fundraiser, so you donate a few dollars.

In the past few weeks, you have now cleaned up your community, provided essential clothing to people in need, and provided an organization with a leg up to make real change in the world. You've also likely met some new people at the beach clean-up or at the very least had a few hours in the fresh salty air. You've cleaned out your closet of clutter. You've provided a better future for yourself and the next generation. It doesn't take much, but it can make real shifts in our lives.

For the past five years, I've done an annual charity cycle ride that benefits rare cancer research through Memorial Sloan Kettering. Yes, I want to see rare cancers knocked out and save countless lives, but the reasons I continue to donate to this particular fundraiser are more selfish. First, I'm working out at a free spin class that kicks my butt each time. Sure, I could donate to Memorial Sloan Kettering directly, but this way makes it more fun for me. Second, if I ever get one of these rare cancers down the road, hopefully there will be some new treatment options to help save my life.

It's okay if the reasons you're donating are less about the world and more about you. It doesn't change the good you're doing in the world. If you're donating furniture to a shelter because you desperately need that hideous chair your mother-in-law gave you out of your house, that's totally fine. You're still helping that shelter out with the furniture they need.

You can also help the world by abstaining from something. Since clothing production causes 10% of human based carbon emissions, you could decide not to buy clothing you know you'll only wear once. Maybe you've committed to not using any plastic bags this year and bringing reusable bags to the grocery store. Both things are still helping the environment stay livable for you as you get older. You're not giving up anything in exchange for getting a healthier planet.

Remember earlier when we talked about *Closing Some Tabs*? This is one of those cases. You don't have to care about all charities in the world. Pick two or three causes that matter to you and then find ways to help those things specifically.

For me, I've chosen:

CYCLE FOR SURVIVAL
A yearly event that raises money for rare cancer treatment research. I participate in their yearly cycling event and raise money through family and friends to "support my team."

THORN
An organization that combats child sex trafficking by building technology used to trace and locate traffickers. Bonus: it's co-founded by Ashton Kutcher, so I occasionally get emails with his beautiful face in them. I donate money or purchase items from their shop to fund their efforts.

SANDY HOOK PROMISE
An organization founded by the parents of the children who died in the Sandy Hook shooting in 2012. Their mission is to reform gun laws in America and I help them circulate petitions, advocate for mental health services in local schools, and send letters to government officials urging them to vote on any upcoming measures.

If you're feeling too overwhelmed by trying to save the world, just pick a couple of causes and focus your efforts there. Not sure where to start? Pick something from the following list and do one of those things before this month is over.

Give It A Fucking Shot

(Pick One)

☐ Donate clothes or household items.

☐ Research an organization or cause you care deeply about and donate either once or monthly to them.

☐ Donate blood.

☐ Volunteer for a food bank.

☐ Do a community clean-up.

☐ Spend your time tutoring or helping children in an underserved community.

☐ Buy gifts from a website that gives a portion of their proceeds to charity.

☐ Drop off old pet items at a local shelter.

☐ Run a 5k that raises money for a cause.

GET A CHECK UP

You're a grown up. I hate to be the one to break this to you, but you're not the shiny new car anymore. You know how I know that? Because you can read this.

As we age, we're slowly deteriorating—but that's depressing, so let's use a car analogy instead.

When you were born, you were the fancy new car, right off the manufacturing line. As you entered childhood, you were the brand-new car, being driven off the lot. Once you enter your twenties and thirties, your warranty starts to go. The paint starts to chip. The tires begin to wear.

Unfortunately, modern medicine as we know it has only been around for a few generations. Unlike a car, the people who are qualified to fix us can't hoist us up on a lift and take out all our insides for days on end to figure out what's going on. There's a lot that medicine still doesn't know, so the sooner we catch things, the easier they are to treat.

Just like you would get a regular oil change or tune-up for your car, get a regular check-up for your body. You're going to have it a lot longer than the piece of metal sitting in your driveway right now.

It's pretty standard to get blood work on these visits. If you're afraid of needles, just breathe and remember it only takes a minute. Keep in mind it's better to do blood work now than to go through treatment for something later. I also find it's really helpful to just have a baseline. If I do blood work every year and suddenly my vitamin D is low and I realize I've been getting migraines recently, I can try taking vitamin D supplements to see if that helps. I might not know my vitamin D levels are low for my range if I don't have prior years to compare it to. I also ask for thyroid checks since my mom had thyroid cancer, and a quick autoimmune panel since I've had issues there in the past.

Most insurance covers a yearly visit for free, so I knock it all out at once. Like I'm prepping for the all-you-can-eat-buffet of medical visits, I make a list of any weird shit that's been happening in the month or so leading up to the appointment and ask it all. Allergies, sore throat, trouble sleeping—you name it. I drove here and sat on a freezing table in a silly gown for an hour—I'm asking everything.

Give It A Fucking Shot

- ☐ Get a yearly check-up. Seriously. Just do it.

- ☐ When you go, ask for a comprehensive blood panel and for the doctor to check your basic vitamin levels and organs. If you have a family history of anything, ask them to check on that stuff, too.

- ☐ If you're a lady, get a pap smear and breast cancer check.

- ☐ If you're a dude, get a prostate exam.

- ☐ Follow up if you don't hear back about your results. Sometimes they get busy and forget to call. It's not a date, you can call them first without it being weird.

VOTE, EVEN IF YOU DON'T CARE

This won't be political. It's not a section where I say, "Vote for this issue", or, "Vote for this person." I promise you; this is just facts.

> Did you know that in Australia it's illegal not to vote? It's called compulsory voting. If you don't vote, they fine you. Even in state or local elections.
>
> Belgium has had compulsory voting since 1893.
>
> In Singapore, if you don't vote, you lose your right to vote in future elections. You're also fined.
>
> There are penalties for not voting in almost two dozen developed nations.
>
> If you don't vote in the United States, nothing happens.

You may miss the opportunity to post an "I voted" sticker selfie on social media. Sure, some family and friends are going to be pissed and make snide comments, but overall, nothing happens. It seems a lot of people think voting is useless and their vote doesn't matter.

But it does matter.

You pay taxes. Everyone does—it's one of the actually compulsory things we're required to do. Don't you want to have a say in how much you pay in taxes? Don't you want to have a say in where your taxes go?

You'll get sick one day. It's going to happen. The human race has a 100% mortality rate so at some point, you'll need health care. Don't you want to have a say in how much someone can charge you to save your life? Or if you're even allowed insurance after someone does save your life? Or if your rate goes up after you've given birth to a different human?

If for no other reason, vote because your friends will know if you don't. There are now apps called "Out Vote" or "Vote with Me" that show you if your friends, acquaintances, and neighbors voted in every election. You can't pretend like you voted when you're in a heated discussion with a friend. This isn't like pretending you didn't vote for Sanjaya on American Idol. They can easily check if you're lying.

Keep in mind that you're voting for more than just the president. In 2016, Californians voted on if porn stars should have to wear condoms when filming. This may not directly affect your life, but there might be stuff on there that does. Your ballot could have a measure on rent control or sales tax increases. You could be voting to legalize shrooms like the people of Oregon did in 2020.

Voting isn't fun for most people. I get that. Neither is going to the DMV to get a driver's license. Neither is getting a credit card or standing in a TSA line at the airport. Hell, the first section of this book was filled with a ton of super un-fun things we do in life. We've just all agreed to do these things because we have to at some point.

This one has just as much of a direct impact on you as all that other shit. I promise.

Also, voting is an open book test. Google some issues, write your choices on a piece of paper, and bring it with you so you don't have to memorize propositions and local sheriff selections. You can even skip some stuff. Don't want to vote for sheriff? Fine. This isn't your high school calculus quiz. You don't get penalized for skipping a few questions.

If you don't want to change out of your pajamas to vote, vote by mail. It's free. I mean, you could probably vote in pajamas at your local polling place, but this way makes it less weird for the other people.

The United States voting system doesn't make sense most of the time. It's very antiquated, like a lot of systems in the world.

But like Nike says, "Just Do It!"

FIND CHEAP STUFF THAT'S WORTH IT

When I was straight out of college, I drove across the country and moved into my first real, grown-up apartment in Los Angeles. The problem was I didn't have a grown-up person budget. I needed all the normal stuff for a first apartment, like a bed, a couch, a dining table, and trash cans. But I was a poor, recent college graduate. How do I afford things like food? How do I get clothes, so people know I clearly belong in my new L.A. lifestyle? How do I get around a city where a gallon of gas is more than a gallon of milk?

I learned a few ways to afford all those things and more. Now it's my turn to share these tricks with you.

FURNITURE AND HOUSEHOLD ITEMS
Go on Craigslist, navigate to the "for sale" section, and type in "moving sale." You'll likely find people moving who are selling things for cheap. This is how I've gotten a one-year-old microwave for $20, free bar stools, a $100 dining room table with chairs, and a fifty-five inch Vizio Smart TV that was three years old for $80. Plus, if you have a big enough car, you can get already-assembled furniture for half the price, saving you from having to flimsily assemble something based on cartoon drawings.

If that's not your thing, try places like Ross, HomeGoods, and TJ Maxx for furniture that's less expensive than pieces at big box stores. They also have pillows, bed sheets, and shower curtains for less than most other places.

GROCERIES

Generic store brands are usually cheaper and the same quality as brand names. I also like going to grocery stores that have rewards programs. Sometimes when you buy three of something, you get the fourth free. Fun trick with those type of sales: you don't always have to buy three to get the discount. For example, four for $8 might just mean each item is $2, regardless of if you buy four.

MEDICINES

Generic medications are often manufactured with the same active ingredients (the ones that matter) as the name brand ones, but they may not have the same inactive ingredients or they're cheaper because they're a different form (fast acting vs. regular tablets). Oftentimes they're exactly the same; you're just paying for the advertising of the name brand.

GASOLINE

There are apps that can help you find cheaper gasoline within a certain radius, like GasBuddy. For example, if you ask the app to "find gasoline stations within four miles," they'll show you every gas station and their most recent prices.

FLIGHTS

First, fly on Tuesdays or Wednesdays. Midweek is cheaper than weekends or near the weekend. Try to avoid major holidays, especially when traveling domestically. The experts say booking forty-eight days in advance (or around there) is a good margin, but there are mixed opinions on that. Just keep checking back.

If you've been searching the same flight a few times and see the price creeping up, lay off for a day. You may be messing with the airlines' algorithm, causing it to think that the flight is suddenly popular. Also try using a different computer or an incognito browser window to see if the price is different that way.

Last tip: Try sites like SkyScanner and Kayak. They'll tell you about current deals on most major airlines.

ONLINE ITEMS

There are a bunch of websites that help you save money. You can install a plug in to your browser, like Honey or RetailMeNot, to scan for coupons. Or you can Google promo codes for a certain company if you ever see a promo code box at checkout. When you sign up for mailing lists, you're usually offered a quick promo code. Try going to Google's Shopping tab when looking for a certain item and see if it's cheaper somewhere else.

EXERCISE

You can negotiate your gym membership, just like everything else. If they won't lower the monthly price, have them waive the initiation fee. You're just paying them to put your name into their database.

If a gym membership is too pricey for you right now, get workout videos for free online. Running outside is free, too. There are easy ways to work out that don't cost a lot.

I also like finding friends who will work out with me. If no one holds me accountable for working out, chances are I'll skip quite a few sessions. You don't need to pay a trainer to keep you honest, just ask a friend or coworker.

RECOGNIZE IT'S JUST STUFF

"It's just stuff." A sentence my mom used to say all the time. When we would talk about what to do if the house was burning to the ground and we had to evacuate quickly, she would say, "Grab the dogs and get out of the house. We can replace the rest. It's just stuff." When I got in my first car accident only a month into having my driver's license and I was scared the car was going to get totaled, she said, "It's just a car. The stuff doesn't matter. What matters is you're safe."

Something about this mentality growing up made me a less sentimental adult about material things. I cherish memories, experiences, and friendships more than anything. I know deep down that everything leaves our lives. When I look at getting gifts for people, I try to find either an event (concert tickets, sports game, day trip) or something that can be used towards an experience. The physical gift I get someone will likely end up in a donation bin within the next decade. What I'd rather give someone is a memory. An experience. I can hardly remember the things I've gotten for birthdays, holidays, or anniversaries over the years. What I can remember is the parties I've gone to, the gatherings to celebrate something, the trips I've taken for birthdays or holidays, and the people I've met along the way.

We have Black Friday and Cyber Monday. We have Labor Day car sales and Memorial Day mattress sales. Half of my inbox is people trying to sell me something. At the end of the day, the stuff gets replaced, lost, breaks, or finds a home somewhere else. We get so lost in the idea of having the next thing that we don't stop to look around at what we already have.

Once you no longer need something, get rid of it. If it breaks, toss it. When you get rid of something, you don't always have to replace it. It's remarkable sometimes how freeing your house of clutter can free your mind of clutter, too. Plus, then you aren't the house on the street with so much stuff that it's spilling into the front yard.

When all the stuff that surrounds you is gone one day, will you even remember you once had it? Much like Blockbuster Video, everything will eventually go away and you'll forget it ever existed. When the people are gone, you'll definitely remember the times you once had with them.

It's all just stuff. What the extreme example of my mother's "in an emergency, don't take stuff" sentiment taught me was that things are replaceable, people are not. Hold onto the people in your life. They are what matters.

LIVE LIKE NOTHING STAYS THE SAME

Can you think of one thing that has ever stayed the same? Your friends. Your home. Your favorite show on Netflix. Every day, every moment is different than the one before. So why do we assume life will stay the same?

We're all on the verge of having our lives change forever and we don't even know when it's going to happen. It's why I save as much money as I can. I'm one bad situation away from being homeless and one good situation away from living in a giant mansion.

Think about it. I'm one bad situation away from going broke—a health problem could eat up my funds and render me unable to work or I could be robbed and have to spend time recovering my losses. Just one moment and I could be sleeping in my parent's guest room, purely because I'm fortunate enough to have parents who have a guest room they'd let me stay in. I'm also one bad situation away from losing my own mental or physical stability, like being a victim of an assault or being diagnosed with a major illness.

Inversely, I'm one great situation away from being a multi-millionaire—I could land my dream job, win the mega millions lottery, or Julie Andrews could come tell me I'm the long-lost Princess of Genovia like in *The Princess Diaries*. It could happen. I just need one moment where my dream comes true and I'll be leveling up in life.

We do everything we can to control these changes and steer life's inevitable shifts in the millionaire direction instead of the homeless direction. Unfortunately, not everything's in our control. When the Covid-19 pandemic hit, everyone was forced to realize that everything they had could go away tomorrow. Our jobs, our money, our health, our security, and our mental stability were all suddenly in jeopardy. What we need now are the tools to help us get through these things. Saving is great for the bank account. Meditation is great for the mind. Tools in general are great at preparing us for life's shifts.

I hate to tell you this, but your life is never going to stay the same. In fact, in a few short hours, days, weeks, or months, it's going to change, and it will never be the same as it is at this exact moment.

I know it's scary but it's also great. Do you wish you still had the life you had when you were twelve? Probably in the carefree-kid way, but not in the life-improvement way. You've learned so much and come so far since those awkward twelve-year-old days.

As we grow and change, so does life. Prepare for life to change. It's the only way we can embrace what's ahead without spending the rest of our lives constantly surprised that time didn't freeze.

Gain the tools you need to adapt for the good *and* the bad. Build a strong network of family and friends. Build strong mental and physical health. You've got this. You've done it before, and you'll do it again.

PRIORITIZE YOUR WANTS

I had a conversation with a friend that went like this:

FRIEND: "I want to quit my job."

ME: "When?"

FRIEND: "Today. I hate it there."

ME: "Aren't you moving in early February? It's only October. You have like ten weeks left before you quit."

FRIEND: "Yeah, but I don't think I can last that long."

ME: "Well what would you do in the time between quitting and moving?"

FRIEND: "I'm not sure."

ME: "Are you making enough at this job to cover your current bills and possibly continue to save for the move?"

FRIEND: "Yeah."

ME: "If you quit, how will you pay rent?"

FRIEND: "I have a good amount of savings."

Quitting is what he wants today. Moving is what he wants in the future. His future self is going to be so pissed at him for his decision to quit. In three months, when he moves, he'll wish he had money for a nicer apartment in the new city, a moving truck, new furniture, and to cover all the unexpected moving expenses we constantly forget about. Instead, he'll have spent a good amount of his savings on three months of rent in a place he moved out of anyways.

He was going to have to figure out which he wanted more—quitting or moving. If he wanted to move in style and get the best possible place in the new city, he was going to have to adjust his priorities and mindset accordingly.

If he goes to work each day thinking, "If today sucks, I'll just quit," then he probably will. Someone will make him upset and, out of an emotional state, he'll say, "Fuck it" and walk out. He'll justify it because he had already acknowledged quitting as an acceptable reaction. If he readjusts his thinking to say, "I'm going to stick this out until January so I can move the way I want," then when someone upsets him at work, he won't quit but will rather think, "I only have a few more weeks here. I can make it." If his dream right now is to move, he should focus on making that dream the best possible version of itself. If he were to compromise on it—like getting a smaller apartment because he didn't save as much as he could have—then realizing his dream may not feel as satisfying.

Give It A Fucking Shot

- ☐ If you're having trouble deciding something similar, write out your current "wants" and rank them.

- ☐ Then let those priorities inform your choices.

BE RELIABLE

You know that friend of yours who always agrees to plans and then cancels last minute? Don't be that friend.

As we get older, people start having less of a tolerance for those people. If you cancel all the time, or even frequently enough that people notice, you'll stop getting invited out.

I recently went to a very popular, way-too-cool-for-me brunch spot that required a reservation. There was a twenty-four-hour cancelation policy, and the restaurant required your credit card to hold your spot. If you canceled or changed your reservation after that twenty-four-hour window, they charged you $25.

I had a few friends I wanted to go to brunch with, but I only invited the ones I knew wouldn't flake out on me. I'm sure the other people would've been amazing to go with, but I couldn't count on them.

The same has been true for friends who are always late. If I'm seeing a show or going to a restaurant, I'll tell certain friends to arrive early in the hopes they'll show up on time. When I'm looking for a low-maintenance night out, I don't invite those friends.

Whether we mean to or not, flaking on plans can become a habit. It often begins innocently enough. We start doing it every so often with acquaintances or gatherings that don't mean that much to us. Then it escalates, and we start flaking on closer friends or a bigger event. Before we know it, we're showing up late to events where our tardiness could get us fired and canceling plans that could cost us friendships.

It's a hard habit to break, but it's an easy one to keep.

Only say yes to plans you know you'll stick to. If you aren't sure, be honest. Instead of saying yes, knowing you might cancel later, say, "I'm not sure about that night, let me get back to you," or, "I understand if you have to go ahead and book it. If I can make it, I'll check in with you to see if someone else canceled."

Keep your word. When you start being the reliable person that everyone can count on, you start getting invited to way cooler shit.

STOP TALKING SO MUCH

"If you want to know what a person is thinking, stop talking." This was advice given to me by my boss when I was twenty-five years old. In previous jobs, I had been told, "You don't have to know everything, you're young." Or, "Listen, you might learn something."

What everyone was trying to say to me was, "You talk too much." It wasn't until I stopped that I noticed how often I was doing it. When we talk too much, or interrupt people, we talk ourselves out of learning something. I found myself cutting people off a lot just to speak, even if it added nothing to the topic. When someone would try to teach me something at work, I would say, "I actually did something similar at my last job." I had to learn to just shut up and let them teach me. Even if I already knew how to do it, I let them teach me anyway. It often spawned other conversations.

Not all things need to be said. We say some things just because we feel uncomfortable with the alternative: silence. Maybe we think that if we're quiet the other person will think we're stupid. Maybe it's nerves. Maybe it's us trying to overcompensate for not knowing something. Maybe we think silence means the other person isn't interested in us. Maybe we think the person we're talking to is struggling to find something to say, too. Whatever the reason, it's a habit we should strive to break.

In my late twenties, I went on vacation with my family. I started noticing at dinner that a family member was averaging about six seconds of silence before she said something. She was often speaking just to fill air and it seemed to be coming from an anxious or energetic place. She was only talking because she wasn't comfortable with silence. She was missing the calm in not having to come up with a conversation starter. The calm that exists once you get used to the silence because you have room for your own thoughts.

Sometimes we get so uncomfortable in silence that we say something just for the sake of saying something. If moments later no one has responded, we regret saying anything at all because now we're sitting in a silence more awkward than the one before.

Have you ever filled a silence with a generic remark like, "The weather has been amazing recently," or, "Did you see the game last night?" only to be met with a, "Yeah," and then more silence? Or perhaps you make a mundane observation about something or someone in the immediate vicinity. "Uh oh, that waiter spilled some water on his shirt," or, "That baby's cute." These are things we say to just fill air.

The consequence is that when we have something important to say, it's diluted. When we're always talking, we train others to stop listening. If we're speaking just to speak, then when we do have something important to say, it gets lost.

Think about recent conversations you've had. How much of the time the other person was speaking were you just waiting to respond? We spend so much of the time that the other person is speaking formulating what we're going to say next instead of actually paying attention to what *they're* saying.

Once when discussing how to navigate a salary negotiation, my dad gave me great advice about listening. He said, whenever someone asks you a question, count to two or three in your head before you respond, even if you know the answer. That way, when you're asked something that stumps you, you don't look like you've been caught off guard. You've established a normal response time.

When I started doing this in meetings, I realized how often I jumped in the moment a person stopped speaking. I started counting to two all the time—in meetings or in social engagements with friends. Before I knew it, I had formed a habit to wait a beat before I responded.

When I'm giving a passionate speech about an important topic, or if I've had a few drinks and am with friends, these practices rarely apply. But knowing I'm able to exercise them gives me a bit more power when it matters most.

Give It A Fucking Shot

- ☐ This week notice how often you interrupt people.

- ☐ Try counting to two in your head before you respond. It's easy to test on a phone call since you can actually set a timer or use tools to assist you.

"WHEN YOU TALK, YOU ARE ONLY REPEATING WHAT YOU ALREADY KNOW. BUT IF YOU LISTEN, YOU MAY LEARN SOMETHING NEW."

— DALAI LAMA

PUT DOWN YOUR PHONE

Did you know that the sound of a text on your phone triggers the same part of your brain as a slot machine? It generates a feeling of instant gratification and is designed to addict us.

One time I was in college and my friend asked me to go to lunch. Almost immediately after we sat down, she took out her phone and started texting her boyfriend. They had a long-distance relationship and her excuse for always being on her phone was that they needed to be in constant contact to feel connected. I had eaten my entire salad before she even looked up. I would ask questions or try to start a conversation and she would half answer, not listen, or give me the "one-minute" finger. After a while I got up and went to the bathroom, and when I came back, she hadn't even noticed I'd left the table. So, I left—for real this time. I got in the car and drove home. It wasn't until nearly fifteen minutes later when I was almost all the way home that she texted me, "Hey, where are you?" I told her I left. "You hadn't said more than ten words to me all lunch—why even ask me to go with you?"

Does this sound like anyone you know? If you're ever in line at a coffee shop, sitting on a subway, in the waiting room at a doctor's office, or even at a red light, look around and see how many people are on their phones. We can't go five minutes in a public space without checking our phones. We've been conditioned to be uncomfortable in public, myself included.

We all think we're good at multitasking but we're usually not. I don't mean the doing squats while brushing your teeth kind of multitasking, but the more dangerous forms, like texting and driving.

My mom is going to hate this story, but I'm telling it anyway. Before Bluetooth, you had to answer the phone and put it on speakerphone in the car. This was the early days of cell phones. She would always have her phone in her purse or her pocket, and when she was driving, she would try to dig around and find it. She would be driving all over the lane while she tried to get her phone out to answer it. I would tell her there's nothing so important that it can't wait until you get to the red light or pull over. She would always say, "What if someone's hurt?" or, "What if it's work?"

To which I would say, "Then they will still be hurt when you call them back in two minutes. You're in a car near no one else, you can't help anyway," or, "If it's work, you'll call them back. You're not the president. No one is calling to warn you about a nuclear bomb attack. It can wait."

If someone died and you're getting a call to find out about it, as tragic as that is, they'll still be dead when you reach your destination. If you kill yourself in a crash trying to answer the call, now there are two dead people.

We all know the dangers of texting and driving, but it's more than that. We're losing our ability to have human interactions. We can no longer just sit with another person in silence. Instead, we have to be doing something—or at least seem like we're doing something—all the time. Sometimes I open my phone to check the time, and don't even register the time once I've put it back down again. That's how routine the concept of just looking at my phone has become.

There are some easy things you can do to break this addiction.

Start small. Don't go throw your phone out of the window. Unless you really want to, then do it. That looks fun. But maybe try the following steps first.

Give It A Fucking Shot

- ☐ Turn on do-not-disturb mode. You can add emergency numbers that can get through with DND on, but otherwise try to set at least a few hours each night of phone-free time.

- ☐ Turn off any notifications you don't need. You can keep voicemail, text, and email on, but turn off the rest. You don't need to know instantly about an Instagram like.

- ☐ Put your phone in a different room during mealtime or family time.

- ☐ Don't bring your phone into the bathroom. No one needs you while you're shitting or showering. Also, bacteria. Gross.

- ☐ Don't text and drive. You can put your phone in the back seat while you drive so you won't be tempted to touch it.

- ☐ Try leaving your phone alone when you do other small things, like walking the dog or doing laundry.

BE MORE INTERESTING

My favorite TV show of all time is *Friends*. I know, it's not at all surprising that a girl in her thirties loves *Friends*. Over the years, I've come across many fellow *Friends* lovers and have asked a lot of them, "Who's your least favorite character?" The overwhelming answer has been Ross.

Of course, people choose Ross; he's so dull and incredibly one note (sorry writers). All he ever talks about is science and divorce. Every joke goes back to those two things.

I almost never hear Monica or Rachel as the answer, and I suspect that's because of variety. They both have careers they're passionate about and discuss readily, but they also have hobbies, personality quirks, and a broader range of interests than boring old Ross.

All of this is to say, don't be the person at a dinner party who always wants to talk about the same thing. We all have that one relative who always wants to discuss politics because they think it makes them sound smart. I always find it's nicer when you find the person at the dinner party who you can talk to about anything. You start your conversation with one topic and within an hour you've covered a dozen things with the same level of enthusiasm.

People who can talk about anything seem inherently interesting. When I first noticed this, I began to have discussions with people about everything, not just things that interested me. If I had a client at work who mentioned they went golfing this weekend, I'd ask follow-up questions. What course do they go to? Do they golf a lot? I have never gone golfing in my life, but this exercise became good practice for being able to talk about any topic with any person. I learned about topics I never thought I would be knowledgeable about, but more importantly, I learned how to carry on a conversation about something I knew nothing about. Now I feel like if I sat in a room with the Queen of England, I could hold a dialogue for an hour without any worries of an awkward silence. HRH Lizzie and I could discuss anything in the world with complete ease.

This method works for awkward dates, too. If I'm on a date with a person, and within five minutes I know there won't be a second date, I still find something they're interested in that I may not know a lot about and discuss that. At least I'll come out of the experience with some new information that may eventually help me have a more stimulating conversation with a person I *am* interested in.

Who wouldn't want to be as interesting as possible? When it comes to public figures, we're typically more entranced with the ones with a varied set of interests. On the surface, Tom Selleck is just an actor, but he becomes more interesting when you learn he also has an avocado farm. Georgia politician Stacey Abrams wrote more than half a dozen romance novels. Michael Jordan played baseball years ago and people still can't shut up about it. These things make them interesting because they're not what we'd expect from them. These well-known figures stepped out of the box and surprised everyone by spicing up their persona with a little variety.

Take this book. If it was all about one thing, would you still be reading it? Honestly, if we had stopped at Chapter One and only talked about savings accounts for the entire book, would you have kept reading? You're reading this book because it offers a range of topics and a variety of ways for you to grow.

So, spice up your life a bit.

Find something outside of what you know and read an article about it. Watch a TV show or documentary you wouldn't otherwise watch. Have a conversation you'd normally walk away from. See what it sparks in you.

SETTLE FOR MORE THAN OKAY

Fun Fact: You're going to settle in your life. Nothing will be perfect 100% of the time. Not everything will be exactly as you imagined it. In fact, most things won't.

Remember how there's no perfect person for you? You're not perfect, either. The things that will come your way will have flaws because everything does. Accepting that is part of life.

Just because you'll settle, doesn't mean you have to settle for just "okay." For some people, okay is perfectly comfortable for them. They have the okay job that brings in enough money to live an okay life with an okay partner in an okay house while they drive an okay car around their okay neighborhood.

I want more than okay for you. Okay is comfort. Once we get comfortable with a life we're fine with, we begin to settle more than we planned. We forget the spark that ignited us to strive for more than okay. The desire to trade in our current circumstances for better ones. To dream of the extraordinary.

Think back to a time when you didn't have the life you have now. When you imagined where you'd be one day, was it different from the life you're living? What did it look like? Is there anything in that dream you settled for that you wish you hadn't? It's not too late. See what you can change. If you dreamed of a house on the beach but settled years ago for a house that's miles from the beach, start looking for a place that's closer and see if moving is a possibility.

If you were unemployed and desperate for a paycheck, so you settled for the okay job, consider looking for something that suits you better. Go after the thing you're most passionate about.

Asking for more than okay means you get a fresh start. It means you get to go back to that dream you once had and reactivate it. Settling isn't game over. You can always play again.

Who says you only get one life? You may only get one lifetime, but that doesn't mean you only get one life. Live lots of lives during your lifetime. Change careers. Move to a new place. Reinvent yourself. Just because you had to settle for something before doesn't mean you're stuck in that thing forever.

A tree grows tall from the place it's planted and grows outward with branches pointing in every direction. You can flourish from the foundation you already have and still branch out into something new.

Keep your dreams alive and remember that you deserve better than okay because you're better than okay. You're awesome.

REMEMBER EVERYONE
MATTERS

I used to work at a company where the owner's daughter would come in sometimes and work from the office. She was the daughter of a multi-millionaire who owned several companies, and she would say "Thank you so much," to everyone.

If someone called for her and she was busy, she would say to the receptionist, "Thank you so much for letting me know. Can you please tell them I'll call them right back?"

If there wasn't an office space for her that day, she would work from the couch in the lobby and thank the office assistant for helping her get set up there.

If she was busy but someone asked her a question, she would pause, make direct eye contact and say, "I'd love to discuss that with you but I'm busy right now. Can I please come find you later?"

She impressed the hell out of me. Her behavior was consistent. It also stood in stark contrast to the behavior of many of my coworkers, who would throw fits if lunch wasn't on time, or would receive messages from reception and walk away without so much as a "Thank you." She was in her mid-twenties, yet she treated people better than most of the middle-aged executives at that company.

Politeness should never be reserved for only certain people. It's free, so give it to everyone.

It doesn't matter who you are because everyone matters. The person who helped ring you up at CVS matters just as much as the doctor who's treating you. Everyone's contributions matter and deserve recognition and appreciation.

Once I was strolling through stores down Melrose Avenue with a friend of mine. We were hopping from clothing store to clothing store, mostly just browsing. By the time we'd made it to our tenth store, we still hadn't bought anything. On our way out, my friend stopped me and asked why I said "Thank you" when leaving every store. "We haven't bought anything," she said. That didn't matter. Whether I bought something or not shouldn't constitute whether I show gratitude. The sales associates were there, ready to help us if we did buy something. I wasn't thanking them for an item, I was thanking them for their hospitality.

A few years later, I was employed at a company where I was in a position of hiring people. I would often stack interviews back to back, every ten to fifteen minutes. I wanted to meet as many candidates as possible to find the perfect person for each position, but my days were quite busy, so I had to schedule the interviews close together.

After all my first-round interviews were conducted, I would make a list of my top candidates. Then I would take their resumes up to the reception desk and ask the receptionist who greeted her kindly, who treated her well while they waited, and even who said "thank you" as they left. If someone was rude to her, or if someone complained about having to wait five minutes past their appointment time, that's what I needed to know.

The people I was interviewing would have to be in the room with clients. If they didn't treat the receptionist with kindness, I couldn't guarantee they'd treat the clients with kindness when I'm not in the room.

It doesn't matter if you're further along in a certain area of your life than someone else. Don't judge those coming up behind you. We were all once them. If you're judging teenagers trying to become Instagram famous, humble yourself by remembering that time your high school band thought they were going to make it big. We aren't better than anyone else.

Didn't we all grow up with the adage, "Treat everyone the way you want to be treated?" It's true. Everyone deserves that. And once you start saying "thank you" more and looking people in the eye when you speak to them, you'll notice how often you didn't do that before.

The eye contact one was big for me. I started realizing I would pick up dry cleaning, run to the bank, and pick up food at a restaurant without being able to tell you what the people who helped me even looked like. It takes two extra seconds to look someone in the eye and make a human connection. Don't just say, "Thank you" to someone; make eye contact and show you're truly thankful.

Gratitude can cause huge shifts in the way we treat people and the way others treat us. Today, try to remember this as you move about the world. See what shifts for you.

And in case no one told you today. You Matter.

DON'T GAMBLE ANYTHING YOU AREN'T WILLING TO LOSE

I'm a terrible gambler. When I go into a casino, I take out $50, $100, whatever I feel is appropriate and play until the money's gone. Usually, that's about half an hour. I told you, I'm a terrible gambler. I basically treat it as if I'm paying for an experience rather than hoping to come out ahead. That's the same for life.

We gamble every day in our lives, but sometimes we gamble with things we can't afford to lose. This can be on a small scale, like if you get a job offer for $10,000 less than you wanted and you tell them that if they don't meet you halfway, you're walking away. That's a gamble; they might let you go. You'll have to find another job, so it has to be a risk you're willing to take. A bigger gamble would be if you've had too much to drink one night and decide to drive home thinking it's fine because you live close. Now you're gambling with your life.

You take tiny risks all day and probably don't even know it: going through the intersection on a yellow light, eating the leftovers from four days ago, dating the guy with nothing but gym selfies on his dating profile.

You've probably gotten used to weighing the pros and cons of each of these scenarios within a split second, so fast you don't even notice it. When you complain to a waiter at a restaurant, you've probably thought for half a second that they might spit in your food, but you decide to do it anyway. Those are the kinds of small risks you're so used to by now, they go unnoticed.

It's when we gamble big that we feel it. The high roller moments. Fighting with your best friend in a major way is gambling that relationship. Investing in a friend's company is gambling on the company, your friend, and the economy in general.

The biggest gambles always involve people. More specifically, they involve the people we care about.

Romantic relationships are nothing but one gamble after another. Reaching for their hand for the first time involves a risk of rejection. Saying "I love you" first is a risk of embarrassment. Moving in together is a risk of commitment. Fighting with them is a risk of losing the relationship. Ending a relationship is a risk that you're making the right choice.

Whether it's an exciting risk or a terrifying risk; it's up to you to make the choice. Only gamble if you're willing to accept any outcome.

STOP COMPARING YOURSELF TO OTHERS

How often do you scroll through Instagram and see everyone's posts about engagements, marriages, babies, whatever, and then getting instantly sad because their life looks more exciting than yours? Darling, that's their life, not yours. Stop comparing yourself to others and more importantly, stop comparing your timeline to the timeline of others. The universe is not in a hurry, you are.

Just because everyone on your feed is having baby number two and you're still single doesn't mean you won't get there, it just means it isn't right for you right now. What's meant to be yours will be if you're patient.

Why do we rush into things that aren't right for us? We think we have to be married because everyone else is, so we rush to find someone, anyone, and just marry that person. That's how divorces happen. You just don't see those things on a newsfeed because they aren't as pretty.

You're doing everything right. You're living life on the timeline you're supposed to. Focus on yourself and what you want. Not everything is right for everyone.

When I was traveling around Vietnam, I spoke to my tour guide about the very riveting topic of wealth disparity and life comparisons. In Vietnam, people tend to make a similar income, have a similar number of children, live in a similar house—so his concept of racing others for what they have seemed foreign. In the moment that I was explaining how everyone I knew was achieving the things

I wanted, I heard how ridiculous I sounded. I don't want Person A's job or Person B's husband, so why am I comparing myself to them? I'm on my own path.

How often have you seen an outfit on someone else, went and bought that outfit, and then been disappointed it didn't look as good on you? That's only because it just wasn't right for you. There's nothing wrong with you or the outfit, you just aren't a match. There are going to be outfits that look better on you than they do on other people. Certain things fit certain people differently—both with outfits and with lifestyles. Not everything is meant for us.

When you scroll through social media and see an amazing announcement from someone, remember that's them at their best. You're probably comparing your worst traits to their best one. Don't peek through a window and assume you're seeing the whole house.

You can't override the mental comparisons by becoming rich and successful. If you have the habit of comparing your life to another's, you'll always find yourself wanting what you don't have. Trust that what you have and what you will have is exactly what is meant for you.

LET TIME SERVE YOU

You have the same amount of hours in a day as Beyoncé. Or Ryan Seacrest. I mean, seriously, how many jobs does that guy have? I'm convinced there are two of him.

You can accomplish everything you want to; you just have to use time as an asset instead of an obstacle. How many times have you said, "I love to do that but I just don't have the time,"? Sure you do. If you plan ahead, you can find ways to make it all work.

Here are some tools that help me.

PLAN YOUR DAY
Find little pockets of time to sneak something in. If you say you never have time to exercise but notice you have thirty minutes free before lunch, go for a walk.

UTILIZE UNINTENTIONAL BOREDOM
When you're stuck on an endless conference call, waiting in a line you didn't intend to spend thirty minutes in, or are trapped on a subway that's running behind, use that time. First, it'll turn your frustration about having your time wasted into a more positive emotion, and second, it'll allow you the chance to be more productive.

Finally make that dental appointment while you're stuck in line waiting for something. Reply to a ton of emails while you're muted on a call. Use that language-learning app you've been ignoring while you're stuck on an unmoving subway.

SCHEDULE RELAXATION

It can be hard to motivate yourself on a weekend but if you have something you really must get done, race for it.

If I have to clean the house, do laundry, pick up dry cleaning, and go to the bank on a Saturday, I usually schedule my relaxation time to start around lunch and then in the morning, I dump a load in the washer, go to the cleaners and bank, come back, switch my clothes to the dryer, and clean the house at a furious pace before the dryer is done.

Time is only wasted if you let it be. Keep your relaxing time—relaxing, and fill your unused time with more productive things.

ASK QUESTIONS

Something really weird happened with the invention of the Internet. People stopped asking questions. At least out loud. They still ask questions all the time to Google, Yahoo, and AskJeeves, if that's still a thing.

As kids we were taught there are no stupid questions, so we asked all of them. Then we asked one question one day and a kid laughed at us and suddenly, no more questions. The embarrassment was unfathomable, and we just knew we could never repeat that mistake again, so we started asking the Internet everything we're too afraid to ask out loud.

That's why we ask really heartbreaking things to Google instead of each other. Did you know in 2019, over 1.8 million people asked Google, "What is love?" We're so scared to talk with others about the meaning of love that we're now Googling it.

Even "What is the meaning of life," cracked the top one hundred questions asked to Google. When we're feeling lost, wondering what it all means, we turn to a search engine instead of each other.

What if we found the courage to ask real people what we have the courage to ask Google? What if we had the conversations we were too scared to have? Imagine the connections we could make and the things we could learn if we just asked.

I mean yes, I need to occasionally ask Google things because no matter how amazing of an answer my friends try to provide, I need the Internet to explain Bitcoin to me.

Siri is really helpful with providing a chicken parmesan recipe or playing your favorite song on repeat for five hours straight, but she can't have a real conversation with you. She can't tell you her thoughts and opinions and she can't tell you personal stories that relate to the topic you're asking about because she doesn't have any. That's what friends and family are for. They go beyond the search bar and make things relatable in a way a computer never could.

For the *real* life questions—for the big stuff—ask *real* people. How many answers in this book would you have already known if you had asked?

Curiosity is power. Be curious. Ask questions. Constantly.

LIVE YOUR LIFE LIKE YOU LIKE IT

You know the feeling in your gut when you make a decision you know is wrong for you? I've made plenty of decisions like that. Drinking more than I should on nights out. Dating people that were definitely wrong for me. Taking on plans I knew I didn't want to participate in.

I'm the only one to blame in those moments. I've been an active participant in my entire life. I've made every decision that led me to this moment. What matters is the balance. Sure, I'm going to fuck up. A lot. But every choice I make has to come from a place of, "Do I like this as part of my life story?" All of it has to lead me to a life I love. No matter the ups and downs, at the end of my life's journey, I want nothing more than to look back and think, "Nailed it."

Self-loathing isn't fun. Rock bottom isn't a cozy shelter from the world. Being stuck in circumstances that you hate isn't a fantastic way to live your life. No one grows up thinking, "I can't wait to be thirty and miserable."

Here's a few thought nuggets to think about.

If you had to write a story about your life right now, how many of the chapters would you enjoy writing? If you knew that someone was going to publish your story at the end of your life, would you change any of the future chapters?

Are you living on autopilot? Are you just going through the motions, eagerly awaiting every Friday so you can get a timeout from your weekly routine?

How many phrases in your life have become routine? "Hi. How are you?"; "Fine, and you?". "Have a great day."; "You, too." Here's a big one that falls into the routine pile—"I love you." We say it at the end of phone calls and before bed instead of just when we really feel it. When's the last time you said, "I love you," to someone because you felt you'd burst if you didn't?

What would you do differently if you started each day of your life like you liked it? Like it was going to be the best day ever?

Instead of saying no to a trip with friends because work might get in the way, I take the trip. My life story deserves adventures more than it deserves overworking. Instead of saying "I love you," like it's a chore to check off the daily to-do list, I genuinely say it when I feel it strongly in my body.

Life's way too short to be stuck on all the things that didn't happen or all the things you could have done. Let that shit go and go live the life you want now.

What would you do differently if you started living your life like you like it?

JUST FUCKING DO IT

When I was younger, like eighth or ninth grade , I went to entrepreneur's camp. I know, my parents had remarkably cool taste in camps. Okay, if you asked them, they would say I picked it out, too, and I did. It was really fun. I made a fake candy business.

One of the first things the camp counselor said was, "The number one reason people fail to achieve their dreams is procrastination."

Okay, sweet. If I want to achieve my dreams, all I have to do is not procrastinate and I can't fail. She didn't say it that way but that's definitely how I heard it. I just needed to stop procrastinating.

We've talked about procrastination a little already: *You'll never have more time than you do right now. What's wrong with right now instead of tomorrow?*

How about this one? If you don't do it, no one's going to do it for you. This isn't fourth grade anymore. You can't bribe little Jonny with a KitKat to make your dreams happen. Stop waiting for something to happen *to* you, and just go make it happen for yourself. Whether we know it or not, we're subconsciously waiting for so many things to just happen.

I can't tell you how many times I go to the fridge, knowing I have nothing to eat in there, hoping something amazing will appear instead of actually going grocery shopping. Not once has cheesecake ever magically appeared (but man, that would be awesome). If you want something, do something to get it.

Emails don't magically answer themselves. Weight doesn't magically fall off your body. Life doesn't magically become extraordinary. We've got to put in the work to make life happen.

We're waiting for someone to knock on the door and hand us our dreams. There are days I'd sit down at my computer and hope that somehow this book wrote a chapter or two while I was asleep. That never happened. I had to write every word.

No one is going to do it for you. But someone else might do it instead of you.

Give It A Fucking Shot... One Last Time

☐   Put this book down.

☐   Go fucking do it.

Acknowledgements

I have a lot of people to thank for making this book happen. In no particular order:

Marc & Louise Sattler, who raised me, supported me, and trusted me to include them in this book without major embarrassment. Everything I am is because of you. Thank you for really nailing that whole raising me thing.

Seth Sattler, for teaching more than I ever thought a little brother could.

Lia Ottaviano, for making my words coherent and organized. Your hard work is so appreciated and your advice is invaluable. You are the best editor a girl could ever ask for.

Matt Young, for using your unfathomable design talent to make this shit look good.

Alejandro Baigorri, for creating a gorgeous cover that even looks great in tiny thumbnails and for being patient with me while I took forever to decide on a font.

Avery Naughton, who provided incredible last-touch editing and double-checked my horrible grammar.

Monica Thompson for proofreading everything before it went out the door.

Andrea Reider, who infused this layout with her professional eye and phenomenal skills.

Kristy S. Gilbert, who was my savior, my genius with an eagle eye, whose contributions I cannot thank enough.

Aubrey LaDuke, Nili Segal, and Sarah Miller, for reading my first draft ever and not judging it hard-core, and for being my cover art decision makers and badass supporters.

Greer Bishop, who has one story in this book, a million stories in my memories, and was taken from this earth way too fucking soon.

Ayn Rand, Chris Brogan, Esther Perel, Dan Savage, Deidre Rae, Karen Salmansohn, and the many others who let me quote them in this book; I am forever grateful to you for giving me permission to include your genius work.

Tim Berners-Lee, Vinton Cerf and Bob Kahn (and probably Al Gore because he talked about it a lot) for inventing the Internet. To all the other people who helped invent it, thank you too. You have all given me valuable resources. Without you this book wouldn't have happened. Or at least it would've taken a lot longer to happen.

Every friend who opened up to me, shared advice with me, and taught me a lesson about life along the way.

Every teacher, mentor and therapist who guided me through life with patience and grace.

And lastly, Kingston for sitting next to me for hours on end while I re-read and edited this book over and over again.

Made in the USA
Las Vegas, NV
29 May 2021